Critical Guides to French Texts

Critical Guides to French Texts

EDITED BY ROGER LITTLE, WOLFGANG VAN EMDEN,
DAVID WILLIAMS

RACINE

Britannicus

John Campbell

Lecturer in French
University of Glasgow

Grant & Cutler Ltd
1990

© Grant & Cutler Ltd
1990

ISBN 0-7293-0316-0

I.S.B.N. 84-599-2930-2

DEPÓSITO LEGAL: V. 249 - 1990

Printed in Spain by
Artes Gráficas Soler, S. A., Valencia

for

GRANT & CUTLER LTD
55-57, GREAT MARLBOROUGH STREET, LONDON W1V 2AY

Contents

Prefatory Note

T H E edition referred to is that of Jean-Pol Caput in the Nouveaux Classiques Larousse series. This and some other editions are listed in the select bibliography at the end of this volume.

References in brackets are either to line-numbers (and never page-numbers) or to act and scene numbers. Italicized numbers in parentheses, followed by page references, refer to numbered items in the bibliography.

I would like to express my appreciation for help given by the Carnegie Trust and the Cultural Service of the French Government. I am grateful to the editors and publishers of *French Studies* for permission to use and amend material published in that journal (see bibliography). Last but not least I would like to thank Elisabeth, Angus, Harry and Noel for their encouragement.

Introduction

B RITANNICUS was first performed in 1669. For the literary historian this is not a minor detail. He or she can describe the state of the French theatre at that time, the development of tragic drama, the rivalry between the young Racine and the experienced Pierre Corneille, the play's cool reception on its first performance (with perhaps the anecdote that it had to compete with a public execution). Most of these facts are fascinating. None falls within the modest ambit of this present work. It asks two simple and therefore very difficult questions: how does the play work, and what is it saying?

Sources have been considered only in so far as they shed light on these questions. There is barely an allusion to traditions, conventions, biography or seventeenth-century history: for all of these, there exist many competent general studies (e.g. *36* and *7*). This absence of comment is not to imply that by a single grand creative fiat Racine drew order from chaos. In the theatre of his own time, as in his own reading, he found dramatic conventions and situations, historical details, a standard form of versification, a certain type of vocabulary even. (See *15* as a good general introduction, and the more detailed *10, 18* and *23*.) Racine is an inheritor. Yet a compilation of this inheritance would no more capture the spirit of *Britannicus* than would an anatomy lesson the living human spirit. *Britannicus* lives. In short, it is a play written to be performed. It was written to give pleasure. These statements might seem gratuitously provocative to those who see *Britannicus* in a different light, whether as a fable of the ego and the libido, crypto-Jansenist propaganda, a record of the struggle between the aristocracy and the rising middle-class, or as a key to poisonous deeds at the court of Louis XIV. The meekness of ignorance demands that such approaches be left to those better equipped to handle them. The aims of this work are deliberately limited but even then, doubtless, absurdly ambitious. If *Britannicus* is to be treated first and foremost as a play, then some attempt must be made to show how through dramatic invention and the resources of language Racine created a tragic action which, three centuries on, can hold, sustain and enlighten us.

The true place of *Britannicus* is in the theatre, being performed before an audience. In reading the play we must try to have the live performance in our mind's eye: tone of voice, visual expression, movement, reactions to what is being said. 'Pour une œuvre dramatique, la vraie vie est sur scène' (*6, p. 793*). Reading a play, however, does have some compensations. We have more leisure to study how it works. How has Racine gone about the subject? How has he transformed a mixture of history and invention into a dramatic plot? What has he made of the historical evidence at his disposal, and how does this relate to the action of the play? By what linguistic means has he sought to serve the dramatic action and heighten our consciousness of what is happening? And, if *Britannicus* is a tragedy, what does that tragedy imply?

1

Subject and Invention

B RITANNICUS is not a work of history, nor is it a 'story'. It is a dramatic creation which uses a well-known story from history. The distinction is fundamental.

The basic elements of the story can be found in historians such as Suetonius (20) and Tacitus (21): the conflict between Néron and Agrippine, the murder of Britannicus, Agrippine's loss of authority and Néron's descent into tyranny. In his historical sources Racine found characters, situations and material details. Clear examples, from Books XII and XIII of Tacitus's *Annals,* are Agrippine's long recapitulation of the events which led to Néron's accession to the throne (Act IV, Scene 2), her threats to Néron's position (e.g. Act III, Scene 3), and the account of the death of Britannicus (Act V, Scene 5). The description of the early part of Néron's reign (Act I, Scene 2) is obviously inspired by a similar account in chapter six of Suetonius's *The Twelve Caesars.* Burrhus's arguments against tyranny (Act IV, Scene 3) are drawn from Seneca's *De Clementia.* A full account of these various sources is given in any scholarly edition of the play. (e.g. *4.* For a summary of changes from text to source, see *37,* pp. 174-80.) Far from seeking to hide his debt to classical writers, Racine goes out of his way to stress their contribution, especially that of Tacitus: 'j'étais alors si rempli de la lecture de cet excellent historien qu'il n'y a presque pas un trait éclatant dans ma tragédie dont il ne m'ait donné l'idée' *(Seconde Préface).* [1]

However obvious the contribution of Tacitus and other writers, we must be careful not to take at face value every-

---

[1] The *Seconde Préface* is the preface of editions of *Britannicus* from 1676. The *Première Préface* is the preface of the 1670 edition.

thing that Racine says in his prefaces. These are primarily
polemical works. The two prefaces to *Britannicus* are no
exception to the rule. When the play appeared it did not
enflame audiences, and its first run was short. Champions of
Racine's older rival, Pierre Corneille, until then the unchal-
lenged master of tragedies set in Ancient Rome, were quick to
point out the liberties Racine had taken with Roman history.
In his prefaces, therefore, the younger playwright set out to
defend his play and, in so doing, to refute alleged deviations
from the historical record. But his words sometimes provide
more heat than light. He proclaims fidelity to history while
accusing the exemplar of his critics of being a worse deviant
than himself. Both accusation and defence now surprise us.
We accept the liberties taken by a writer as part of what is
called creative freedom.

A dispassionate comparison of text and sources shows that
Racine is guilty as charged of departing from historical fact.
His play is a fabrication. This deed he accomplished by
means of selection, modification and invention. From the
mass of historical details at his disposal he picked only those
which suited his chosen perspective: the murder of Britannicus was only one of a multitude of monstrous acts ascribed
to Nero. In his selection Racine was not merely concerned
with the rules of propriety, *les bienséances.* He was patently
interested less in the recording of historical facts than in
re-enacting how the passions may drive human beings
beyond humanity. The abduction of Junie and the murder of
Britannicus are sufficient to provide the causal link from man
to monster.

Much of what Racine borrowed he also transformed.
Seneca's *De Clementia,* for example, was written after the
death of Britannicus. The treatise, with its praise of Nero's
innocence and exhortations to loyalty, was written as propaganda by a political speechwriter (see *11,* p. 77). From it
Racine extracted Seneca's appeal that a ruler seek security in
the love of his subjects, and placed it in the mouth of a brave
soldier who was striving to prevent the murder of Britannicus. A comparison of text and source shows the major
transformations Racine effected in that soldier, Burrhus (as in

the Narcissus of Tacitus). This is a striking example of how borrowed names garb characters whose reality depends entirely on the demands of the dramatic action.

Racine's greatest infidelity to history lies undoubtedly in the creation of Junie. Despite his ingenious or disingenuous disclaimers, the character is a complete invention. A glance at the play suffices to show how important the invention is. Consider the opening situation, conveyed in Agrippine's outrage at Néron's behaviour:

> Il sait, car leur amour ne peut être ignorée,
> Que de Britannicus Junie est adorée:
> Et ce même Néron que la vertu conduit
> Fait enlever Junie au milieu de la nuit.
> Que veut-il?   (51-55)

The focus here is not on Roman history, on a 'slice of life' of the court of the Emperor Nero (as suggested by *46*, p. 276), but on relationships. This initial situation abounds with dramatic potential. For the dramatist it is the springboard of the plot. It leads to a quickly-developing set of conflicts which form the dramatic structure of the play. Both situation and development are radically new. Racine, through the creation of Junie, shifts the centre of interest from purely historical and political elements to the blinding effects of the passions. Néron's passion for power is one with his passion for Junie. The linking of the two gives the tyrant's lust for domination a more immediately human and universal significance.

Dramatist and historian play with the same figures, but it is not the same game. They have different aims. The function of the dramatic poet, in Aristotle's words, 'is to describe, not the thing that has happened, but a kind of thing that might happen, i.e. what is possible as being probable or necessary' (*8*, Ch. IX). For Racine, history is a means, not an end. Nero was known to have been a cruel tyrant who escaped his mother's domination and murdered the son of the previous Emperor. This public knowledge Racine could not change, any more than Shakespeare could change the destiny of

Antony or Cleopatra. But within this necessary restriction he
was free. And the freedom was immense. The playwright
imagined a possible human situation and then constructed a
plot which brings us credibly and dramatically to the catastrophe. In so doing, through the medium of poetry, he brings
us to a heightened awareness of the tragic universe. The first
great witness to Racine's invention is thus the plot. We must
now examine its testimony.

2

Plot

TRAGEDY is not a series of character-studies but, in Aristotle's celebrated definition, 'the imitation of an action' (8, Ch. VI). That action we experience, we have in our mind's eye, as we watch or read the play. The tragic action sets out to arouse emotions, especially those of pity and fear, through a combination of incidents which would not necessarily touch our imaginations unless so combined. The 'plot' is the name we give to that artificial combination. Artifice, of course, will always shock the pure at heart, or the naive. An example of such a reaction, quoted by the actor and producer Louis Jouvet, is Alfred de Vigny's disillusioned comment that a play is something noble which becomes mechanical, 'une pensée qui se métamorphose en machine' (12, p. 21). Jouvet seized on this statement to make an essential distinction between the action of a play (la pensée) and its plot (la machine): 'Ce qui, en effet, intéresse le spectateur, dans une pièce véritable, est bien en dernier ressort la pensée ou les pensées qu'elle suscite dans son esprit; mais c'est à travers une véritable machine que ces pensées naissent, s'installent, et se développent' (ibid.).

Plot is a four-letter word. This is only appropriate for a term which, in certain academic studies of Racine, is never mentioned. But this polite aversion is strange. For Aristotle, plot was the 'the life and soul' of tragedy (8, Ch. VI). A plot is to a play what an engine is to a car. We usually hope to travel without worrying how: we sit back and enjoy the play. But if ever we should ask how the movement was achieved, then we must open the bonnet and examine the plot. For the plot is 'une véritable machine'. It moves the play forward, from opening situation to conclusion. It is the way in which the playwright arranges the incidents of a story (here, the murder of Britannicus) in the order best calculated to achieve the greatest possible impact.

Plot is therefore in the service of the tragic action just as are language, character, costume or scenery. But it is by far the most important servant. As spectators our keenest wish is only too human: to know what is going to happen, to discover what is really going on, to get to the truth. We wish to know even if we have seen the play a dozen times. In this paradox lies the whole power and pleasure of the dramatic illusion. The dramatist plays on our desire to know. And so through the plot he creates suspense and surprise, reversal and irony. For Racine, as a tragic dramatist, this could not have been easy. For he had to steer clear of both the predictable and the arbitrary in his plotting. The emotional impact is obviously more intense if, in Aristotle's words, events 'occur unexpectedly and at the same time in conse-quence of one another' (*8*, Ch. IX). The effect of surprise is the greater if the surprising event is seen to be a consequence of what has gone before. The effect of a reversal of intention is enhanced if, after the event, we can see how it springs inevitably from what was originally intended. Irony, too, springs from our knowledge and lack of knowledge: we see what characters cannot see, and words can be spoken in ignorance of their true significance.

All of this implies what became one of the hallmarks of the French classical theatre: the construction of a plot in which, as Racine himself states, conflicts arise and are re-solved by nothing extraneous to 'les intérêts, les sentiments et les passions des personnages' *(Première Préface)*. Detail is excluded which does not relate directly to the tragic conflict, and there is an absence of physical action. The focus is on the passions and their destructive consequences. Paradoxically, a common Anglo-Saxon reaction (voiced strongly in France in the heady years of the Romantic Movement) has been to spurn this form of tragedy as 'too intellectual'. No porter or gravedigger here! This hostility is understandable. Racine is an unfamiliar potion for imaginations weaned on Shake-speare. But before passing judgement we should remember

William Hazlitt's advice for travelling abroad, 'to take our common sense with us, and leave our prejudices behind'. [2] In French classical tragedy (as indeed in Shakespeare) thought and emotion interfuse as hydrogen and oxygen in the air. Only by analysis can we reduce them to separate elements. 'Our emotions in the theatre, far from driving out thought and meaning, are indivisible from them; they are simultaneous and mutually dependent. The experience of tragedy can achieve this coherence in a way that the emotional experiences of real life generally cannot because they are too close, too cluttered with detail and partiality, to be seen in perspective.' [3] Exclusion of the contingent means concentration on the essential. The elimination of everyday details and physical action allows a more powerful beam of interest to search hearts and minds, emotions and reactions. The construction of the tragedy and its language are designed to arouse emotions which heighten our awareness of what we can only call the human condition. The logical ordering of the plot itself mimes the inescapable nature of human passions. This is the air we breathe when we see or read *Britannicus,* not some rarefied ether of the intellect.

Racine sets out therefore to link together a series of events both unexpected and necessary, which develop from the situation exposed at the beginning of the play. These events will unfurl in a wave of rising emotion, till the final reversal sends human desire and passions crashing to the shore, where they are revealed for what they are.

A play has, in Aristotle's deceptively simple words, a 'beginning, middle and end' (*8,* Chap. VII). Each of these phases is important in its own right.

---

[2] *The Complete Works,* ed. P. Hull (London, Dent, 1930-34), 21 vols, Vol. X, p. 89.

[3] Oliver Taplin, 'Emotion and meaning in Greek tragedy' in *Oxford Readings in Greek Tragedy* (Oxford University Press, 1983), p. 11.

The Beginning

Given the demands of the plot, the exposition must satisfy
two sets of apparently contradictory criteria. In the first,
instance, it must provide us with the basic facts we need to
know in order to follow the play, yet it must do so naturally,
as part of the dramatic action. A play begins at the beginning.
It falls flat on its face if characters have to spend time telling
each other woodenly who they are, where they are and what
they are doing there. Secondly, the exposition must give us
the elements from which the play will develop, yet still
reserve possibilities of suspense and surprise.

In this light, the exposition of *Britannicus* shows us a
young playwright who is already master of his craft. At the
beginning of the play we expect facts. Racine begins with
emotion: 'Quoi?' Albine is surprised to find, at daybreak, the
Emperor's mother waiting alone in front of the closed door of
her son's private apartments. In Agrippine's response there
spills out the worry, frustration and anger which Néron is
causing her. The dramatic action thus begins with the first
words which are exchanged. It is dramatically necessary that
Agrippine should explain to an astonished Albine the reasons
for her presence and the emotions caused by Néron. Thus it
is in the most natural of ways that we learn the identities and
relationships of the main characters, as well as the conflicts
which oppose them. The germ of the play's development is
expressed in these first few lines:

> Contre Britannicus Néron s'est déclaré;
> L'impatient Néron cesse de se contraindre.   (10-11)

The explanation of this statement leads to the news of Junie's
abduction by Néron, and the revelation that he has been
slowly stripping Agrippine of her power, while refusing to see
her alone. Agrippine's desire that Néron should explain his
behaviour is not just an expository technique. It is one of the
main structuring forces in the play ('je le poursuivrai d'autant
plus qu'il m'évite', 123), leading to the 'explanations' of
Act IV, Scene 2 and Act V, Scene 6. With hindsight we can

see how Agrippine's intention ('De son désordre, Albine, il faut que je profite', 124) prepares an ironic reversal.

Throughout the first act there is great stress on secrecy and appearances. Néron is hidden from view: 'César pour quelque temps s'est soustrait à nos yeux' (134). It has been impossible for his mother to discover what he thinks or desires: 'Sa réponse est dictée, et même son silence' (120). Burrhus gives impressions of Néron's rule and provides ideas as to Néron's desires which are totally at variance with the picture presented by Agrippine. She may of course be motivated by spite and jealousy, but then Néron has abducted Junie. Where is the truth? From the very beginning our minds are directed to a process of discovery.

The first act sketches in the political background to the play. But once more the emphasis is not on facts but on a situation full of uncertainties and thus dramatic possibilities. Questions are placed in our minds. Why has Néron abducted Junie? 'Que veut-il? Est-ce haine, est-ce amour, qui l'inspire?' (55). Is this act a sign of tyranny? Or is it, as Burrhus suggests, 'l'effet d'une sage conduite' (131)? Will Néron be an Augustus or a Caligula (32-42)? Is it true that Agrippine 'promet par-delà son pouvoir' (250)? Will either Agrippine or Britannicus regain the power they have lost? Can they ever unite, enemies that they are, to thwart Néron's plans (307-10)? What threat do they pose as they meet together with Pallas (304)? Is there truth in Britannicus's complaint that he is surrounded by 'des amis vendus' chosen by Néron to spy on his innermost thoughts (329-32)? If so, how will this affect the outcome, and what light does this cast on Néron's *Empire?*

It will be noted that these questions placed before us are set in a dimension which is not only political but personal. Britannicus is spurred to action by the abduction of the woman he loves (290-98). Agrippine's desire to hold the balance between Britannicus and Néron reveals her fear of something in Néron about to be unleashed: 'Je le craindrais bientôt, s'il ne me craignait plus' (74). This personal dimension prepares us for the introduction of Néron and Junie, while enabling Racine to hold these characters back until the following act. In this way he can reserve the surprise of what really motivates Néron.

The personal and political conflicts exposed in Act I raise wider questions, connected with the exercise of power, questions of fundamental significance for the tragedy as a whole. Here again the important word is 'question'. What is the nature of the power which Agrippine has lost (111), and which Néron is beginning to wield? Can the Emperor be, as Burrhus compliantly suggests he is, 'le maître du monde' in a state overflowing with 'liberté' and 'vertu' (180-214)? Or must total power necessarily be exercised through fear, as is implied elsewhere (12, 33, 74, 253, 293)? Britannicus and Junie are defined by their 'misère', 'douleurs' and 'malheurs'. Does this weakness stand without defence against Néron's strength? All these questions place the political action and personal relationships in a moral perspective, which, again, is inevitably linked to a process of discovery. At the end of Act I our uncertainties are not limited to the fate of characters.

THE MIDDLE

In the three middle acts the various strands of conflict exposed in Act I are inextricably entangled, and twisted tight by passion into a knot of interests and obstacles. The dramatic tension gradually increases, as one by one possible escape-doors are blocked off and a final confrontation looms. That we cannot predict the outcome does not banish our growing sense of impending catastrophe. Conversely, this sense does not lessen the tension, or imply any 'fatalism'. Indeed, the equilibrium between ignorance and foreboding provides for the proper tragic use of suspense and surprise, in a way always shot through with irony. We are caught up in the action with the characters. We share their emotions and thus, to some extent, their blindness (*25*, p. 131).

The second act opens with Néron. The first image he projects is that of a strong but prudent and caring ruler, expelling Pallas for the public good, to stop him poisoning the minds of Agrippine and Britannicus. The verb 'empoisonner' which Néron employs here (363) will seem in Act V a richly ironic indication of his care. This first image of reasonableness is shattered in the next scene with the revelation of Néron's love: 'J'aime (que dis-je aimer?) j'idolâtre Junie' (384). Some measure of the surprise this creates is the incredulous reaction of Narcisse: 'Vous? [...] Vous l'aimez?' (383-85). The disclosure completely overturns the idea that Néron's political acts have merely political motives. Junie is no longer a source of opposition to be silenced but a love to be won. Britannicus is no longer just a dynastic rival, to be 'protected' from political seduction by the banishment of those near to him: he is a rival in love. We see that Néron has now an even more pressing reason to find a final solution to the problem posed by the existence of Britannicus. His description of Junie's arrival in the palace (385-408) invests with a striking intensity the whole interplay of personal conflicts which provides the framework for the plot. From this moment on the play is a trial of the passions. The revelation of Néron's love has important implications. Agrippine, Burrhus and Britannicus are now in different ways seen as obstacles to Néron's desire. Can the obstacles be removed? Can Néron do what he wishes? Can one man be so powerful as to have all that he desires? The early developments of the plot allow some of the central tragic questions already to take shape in our minds.

A further surprise in Act II is our discovery that Narcisse is betraying Britannicus for Néron's sake (513). This detail adds another element of uncertainty to our perception of the developing situation. Narcisse plays an important role as the mirror of Néron's desires, articulating the unexpressed, always ready with a corrosive 'why not?' to challenge any potential obstacle to their fulfilment: 'qui vous arrête?' (460). Crucially, Néron does not see these obstacles in moral terms. If he is running away from Agrippine, it is to be free from her (507-08), and thus be free to do what he wishes. The question naturally arises: what will happen when he can flee no longer, but would still be free? Only the final act will give the answer.

The following scene (Act II, Scene 3), the first and last
time that Junie and Néron meet alone, adds another twist to
the plot. The helpless captive refuses the advances of her
all-powerful captor (a similar situation is presented in Racine's previous tragedy, *Andromaque*). But Néron has overlooked one obstacle: the potency of the shared fragility of
Junie and Britannicus. When Junie declares that her love
finds its strength in her lover's weakness (645-48), we realize
that this love can only be fortified by any move on Néron's
part to undermine still further the position of Britannicus.
The obstacle is the more formidable for Néron in that he is
blind to its implications. He has all power, but can seemingly
do nothing. His disarray is manifest in the language of the
scene. Compare, for example, the dignity and icy control of
Junie ('De grâce, apprenez-moi, Seigneur, mes attentats', 538)
with the unstable compound of *précieux* love-vocabulary and
scarcely-veiled threats which constitute Néron's response
(539-52).

In this scene Junie makes it clear that Néron's kingdom is
not for her (631-32), and that he has no place in her world
(643-58). This enlarges the moral perspective suggested in the
exposition. It is not just two people who are in conflict. It is
two kinds of authority, the one political and the other moral.
One has its roots in absolute worldly power, while the other
in its very powerlessness seems to transcend that world: 'le
ciel connaît, Seigneur, le fond de ma pensée' (627). The
whole scene is thus of fundamental importance for the evolution and ultimate significance of the tragic action.

The scene also arouses suspense. For Néron decides to
remove Britannicus from the path of his desires by an
apparently subtle ruse. He orders Junie to banish her lover
from her sight. When Britannicus and Junie meet (Act II,
Scene 6), Néron savours the pre-ordained torture by spying
on the whole scene. Junie's necessary coldness, by throwing
Britannicus into a state of confusion, amplifies the uncertainties of the situation. Néron's imperial strategy has narrowed
to the fuelling of his rival's jealousy in order to satisfy his
own: 'Par de nouveaux soupçons, va, cours le tourmenter'
(754). At the end of Act II Néron's desire has surfaced as a

primitive, relentless force. The development of the plot causes us, again, to ask certain questions at this point. How far will Néron go to satisfy this desire? Can it be satisfied? Can anyone or anything stand in his way?

At the beginning of Act III Burrhus tries to halt Néron in his tracks by appeals to will-power. These Néron brushes aside. Burrhus's reminder that Agrippine 'est toujours redoutable' (768) prepares her first appearance since Act I. It is evident that she is counting on her memory of shared crimes to bring Néron to heel (849-54): the credibility of the weapon is discounted by Burrhus. It is equally clear that she is motivated by passion rather than a tardy sense of justice (872-75). For her, Junie is 'une rivale' (880). The mixture of jealousy, spite and wounded pride which this prospect reveals ('Elle aura le pouvoir d'épouse et de maîtresse', 888) adds another dose of volatility to the already unstable situation created by the rivalry of Néron and Britannicus. The effect is increased by the news which Britannicus brings of the mounting opposition to Néron (Act III, Scene 5).

These last scenes of Act III are an important hinge in the plot. For it is here that Britannicus makes a series of mistakes. Firstly, in natural but disastrous ignorance of the consequences of his act, he reveals to Narcisse the details of a possible conspiracy. Secondly, he assumes that he can make common cause with Néron's mother (895-906), despite knowing that it was she who deprived him of the throne. Then, in an unexpected meeting with Junie (Act III, Scene 7), he accuses her of having surrendered to Néron, of being dazzled by 'l'éclat d'un empire' (973). The irony is, that this 'éclat' is specifically what she has rejected. We should not overlook the errors made by Britannicus in his blindness, if only to correct the impression that he is an innocent victim offered for sacrifice. He makes the mistake of believing too readily what he is told by those with no love for him, and of disbelieving Junie. What happens to him is in some measure a consequence of this mistake. Racine speaks in Aristotelian terms of those tragic characters 'dont le malheur fait la catastrophe de la tragédie' *(Andromaque, Première Préface):* 'il faut qu'ils tombent dans le malheur par quelque faute qui les

fasse plaindre sans les faire détester'. It will be noted that
Racine uses the term 'faute' rather than 'défaut'. Britannicus
falls because of something he does, not because of what he is.
The tragedy is not a character-study: it is the imitation of an
action. That the consequences of Britannicus's 'faute' are out
of all proportion to the act he commits can only arouse in us
emotions of terror and pity. Such is the tragic universe. We
are brought to a heightened awareness of its terrifying implications not through some psychological meditation but
through the very structure of the plot.

The meeting between Britannicus and Junie is an astute
dramatic stroke. We know (956) that an alarmed Narcisse has
gone to warn his master that the two lovers are together. We
remember Néron's injunction to Junie that she avoid the
slightest sign of love for Britannicus (683-84). As the lovers
speak, we realize that Néron will soon burst in. A scene
which could have lowered dramatic tension is thus used to
increase it. And so is precipitated the long-delayed confrontation with Néron which both Agrippine (926) and Junie
(1017) have urged Britannicus to avoid.

This confrontation is the only time the two rivals are on
stage together. At their next meeting, Néron will poison
Britannicus. The explosive nature of this first clash prefigu-
res what will happen in the second. The dialogue between
might and right, power and authority, for the first time here
comes out into the open. This scene (Act III, Scene 8) quickly
becomes a sharp verbal duel, a series of wounding one-
sentence thrusts, in which Néron's increasingly open threats
meet Britannicus's ever greater freedom of speech. The arrest
of Britannicus is a climactic *coup de théâtre*. The development is unexpected, yet totally within the logic of Néron's
passion. This arrest, followed by Agrippine's confinement to
the palace and the threat to Burrhus for his critical remarks
(Act III, Scene 9) is the natural outcome of Junie's abduction
at the very beginning of the play. We see that power, if it be
absolute, must silence what opposes it, and crush what will
not fear it. But since the extent of a dictator's power comes
from the fear he arouses, the need to silence opposition
suggests that the power of Néron is far from complete. Act III

therefore concludes with a delicately-poised situation, full of dramatic potential. Each of the characters is isolated. It has been one of the functions of the plot so to isolate them, to make them face up alone to their tragic dilemma. Britannicus, Junie and Agrippine are guarded by Néron's soldiers, while Néron himself, in all the assertions of his strength, cannot impose his wishes on the weakest of them. Junie has offered to sacrifice herself for peace, by becoming one of the Vestal Virgins (1075-76). Néron dismisses an idea he cannot understand. There seems no way out. Each conflict has reached a critical point. We know that something will give, but have no idea what.

The first element to change is Néron's refusal to see his mother. From the beginning she has sought a meeting, to accuse Néron face to face of all that she reproves in his actions. Now it is she who must defend herself against the charge of conspiracy. Burrhus makes her position clear: 'Defendez-vous, Madame, et ne l'accusez pas' (1106). But from the opening lines of the confrontation-scene (Act IV, Scene 2), it is Agrippine who assumes the role of prosecutor: 'Approchez-vous, Néron, et prenez votre place' (1115). As before, her main weapon is memory. She uses her knowledge of the past to show that everything she has ever done has been for her son. In so doing she completely shatters Néron's political legitimacy. But she also gives him a lesson in the treacherous ways of keeping power. Néron's promise of 'fidélité' to his mother (1226) has an ironic double edge. This long scene, far from being some static history lesson, or tame transliteration from Tacitus, is a good example of how a dramatist can exploit mounting emotional pressure. From beginning to end its substance is emotional conflict. This gives a sharp focus to the wider dimension. For what is at stake is the fate not just of Agrippine, but of Britannicus, Junie, the Roman Empire and thus of what we are always tempted to call the civilized world (cf. 1646). One question, which has been hanging over the play since the opening scene, is about to be answered: how will Néron decide to govern? Néron promises reconciliation. It is an unexpected twist to the plot.

Any risk that the emotional intensity will now diminish immediately disappears, as the plot is given yet another twist. Néron informs Burrhus that his words of peace were a sham, that he intends to murder Britannicus, and so be rid of Agrippine's influence too (1314-22). But then Burrhus's passionate defence of clemency seems to touch Néron (1381), who promises he will see Britannicus so as to make a real peace between the rival princes.

It is at this critical moment that Narcisse enters. What follows (Act IV, Scene 4) is a classic temptation scene. 'A spectator is bidden to watch the approach of disaster, to see each step heading up to it, and finally to be impatient for its coming. In other words, the temptation scene becomes a scene that is positively demanded by the action of the play or, what is really the same thing, by the aroused expectation of the spectator' (*19,* p. 93). Narcisse shows Néron that he must poison Britannicus to be free for good (1401-79): Britannicus will be even more dangerous now since his ignominious arrest; Junie will have to be given back to him; Agrippine has been boasting of her easy triumph; the Romans are fickle, secretely crave enslavement and are ready to justify any deed done in their name; as for Burrhus and other high-principled advisors, such people only want power. The arguments are the more perverse for having some foundation in reason. Why then, concludes Narcisse, does Néron not silence them all? Act IV ends in uncertainty. But we cannot help having the feeling, a feeling strengthened by the weakness of Néron's rejoinders, that he has been swayed by the arguments of Narcisse, indeed, that these arguments are his own secret thoughts. Now the whole course of events turns on Néron's decision. Will he take the advice of Agrippine and Burrhus, or follow the call of desire? The knot of conflict is tied tight. Only Néron can now begin to undo it, or cut it through. It is time for the denouement.

THE END

We have seen how the opening scenes of the tragedy posed a certain number of problems in terms of conflicts and obstacles. In the middle, these conflicts have been sharpened and obstacles hardened, as the full tragic implications of the problems are exploited. In the end, or denouement, the obstacles are removed and the conflicts resolved, in a final reversal. This reversal brings with it, for us, a new awareness of the true dimension of the tragic action. The end of *Britannicus* is thus a time of reversal and discovery. It is the moment of truth, shot through with irony.

The denouement begins with an event which at first defies our expectations. Britannicus informs Junie that Néron has abandoned his designs on her and is even now waiting to see him, for a public celebration of reconciliation. It is the first moment of hope for the young lovers. Or rather, it should be. For in that same wave of enthusiasm which carries Britannicus blindly forward, there is a strong undercurrent of fear and treachery which Junie feels and which we cannot but experience. The sense of danger is aroused by Néron's reported desire to embrace Britannicus (1482). We remember the mortal threat of such a promise (1314). Can Néron abandon Junie so easily? Unspoken fear shows in Junie's lack of response to Britannicus's joy. The fear first surfaces as something irrational (1503-04), then as a series of questions which can only intensify the impression that all is not as it seems (1506-34). Can Néron be trusted? Can Narcisse? Is such a sudden change credible? Do promises have the same weight for Néron as for Britannicus? Words such as 'craindre', 'trahir' and 'haïr' recur throughout the scene, in counterpoint to Britannicus's happiness, sounding a warning whose music reaches a crescendo in Junie's admission of sheer fear:

> Tout m'est suspect: je crains que tout ne soit séduit:
> Je crains Néron; je crains le malheur qui me suit. (1537-38)

What if the two lovers were caught in Néron's snare just when they seemed to be, for the first time, free? The interplay of blind trust and gnawing fear is a masterly exercise in plot-construction. It heightens tension by creating a growing sense of foreboding. The whole scene is charged with a pathos poignantly expressed in Junie's stabbing final cry: 'Et si je vous parlais pour la dernière fois!' (1546).

Now the tempo, already urgent ('Il faut partir', 1561), suddenly accelerates. Agrippine arrives to tell Britannicus that he must rush ('que tardez-vous?' / 'Partez en diligence' / 'Néron impatient' / 'Ne faites point languir...' / 'Allez...', 1563-68). Time has run out. And now events seem to be beyond the control of the participants. This is yet another factor which creates pathos. The dramatic machine, so tightly wound up, now unwinds at speed and nothing can arrest it. This movement is hidden, and seemingly halted, by Agrippine's boasts of new-found power. But it re-emerges, quickening, when a rising tumult offstage dissolves her claims in irony. The movement finishes with a series of short bursts (Act V, Scene 4), and the news that Britannicus is dead.

Burrhus's description of the assassination (Act V, Scene 5) has been criticized as the substitution of a static form for a highly theatrical one. Is Racine here not just tamely following the prescriptions and conventions of the contemporary theatre, that no violent action take place on stage? Could he not have added drama by presenting the whole banquet-scene, and so putting on stage the moment of murder, as Shakespeare would have done? Take *Macbeth,* for example!

Take *Macbeth.* It is an instructive pleasure to see how Shakespeare focuses essentially not on violent action, but on reactions to it, on its unhinging effects, e.g. 'Will all great Neptune's ocean wash this blood / Clean from my hand?' (Act II, Scene 1). The conventions Racine exploits (or is subject to, depending on one's point of view) are visibly different from those of Shakespeare. But the tragic focus is the same. There is firstly, of course, the dramatic ploy of keeping Junie, Agrippine and the spectators in ignorance of what is happening. The description of the murder of Britannicus is exploited to stress the quasi-sacrilegious nature of a communion defiled (1625-28), the composure of Néron (quickly imitated by courtiers), and Burrhus's own realization of illusion.

From the play's first appearance, the final two scenes have also attracted criticism. Can one not say, along with Racine's detractors of that time, that 'la pièce est finie à la mort de Britannicus' *(Première Préface)*? This really depends on whether we consider *Britannicus* to be something more than the story of Britannicus. History or tragedy? The question will be discussed in greater detail in the following chapters. Suffice to say here that in the exposition there began a process of exploration, connected with the power of passion and the limits of power. In the last scenes we come to a discovery which is an essential part of that tragic exploration. As Racine suggests, in reply to his critics, we, as spectators, need to see where the characters are brought as a result of their actions. In these final scenes the murders of both Agrippine and Burrhus are predicted (1699-1701). Both in different ways have responsibility for Néron's rule. For Néron the wheel is seen to have come full circle, from the 'empereur parfait' (26) to the bloody tyrant whose murders are self-defeating, and whose suicide is predicted (1687-90). The last words addressed to Néron, Agrippine's 'Adieu, tu peux sortir' (1694), strip away the last vestige of his authority. His desire to possess Junie suffers the ultimate reversal, as she flees to the Vestal Virgins: 'sans mourir elle est morte pour lui' (1722). Néron has intended to seize power in its totality. But the murder of Britannicus causes the flight of Junie and the death of Narcisse. The Emperor is left wandering the streets, alone, mad, powerless to act and, though ready to kill again, yet defeated.

In this reversal we discover that the human condition imposes limits for the man who seeks to play the part of God with other men. That discovery does not come to us through 'the story of Britannicus' but through the play, *Britannicus*. The effect of the play depends in great part on an artificial construction we call the plot. Through an arrangement of different elements of the story, the plot generates a dramatic action which stirs our emotions, moves us to pity and fear, and allows us to taste the mysterious pleasure of tragedy.

3

History and Time

I F we accept the importance of situation and plot in any evaluation of *Britannicus,* and can gain some idea of Racine's inventiveness in these areas, then it becomes difficult to see the play as a mere depiction of life or chronicle of events in Ancient Rome (and still less, in the France of Louis XIV). Indeed, Racine insists that his prime concern is with a set of relationships: 'il ne s'agit point dans ma tragédie des affaires du dehors. Néron est ici dans son particulier et dans sa famille' *(Première Préface).* This corresponds to Aristotle's advice that the tragic deed be done 'within the family' *(8,* Ch. XIV).

A question then naturally arises: what role is played by history? Is the 'Roman' element mere decoration, to add a dignified cardboard setting to a family quarrel? Is it just a sop to the expectation that the subjects of tragedy be drawn, as Aristotle suggested, from 'traditional stories' in history or mythology (ibid.)? The first step towards an answer to these questions is perhaps to look carefully at the 'Roman' elements in the play.

Two different kinds of historical references are to be found in *Britannicus.* There is firstly what could be termed the vocabulary of Roman life, as in 'le peuple au Champ de Mars nomme ses magistrats' (205). Secondly, there is an abundance of allusions to what one might call past history, that is, to historical events preceding the short day of the dramatic action. An examination of both sets of references will give us a clearer idea of how Racine exploited the historical details at his disposal. It will inevitably lead to an assessment of the relationship between the evocation of history and the present time of the developing tragic action.

Britannicus is set in the early part of the reign of the Emperor Nero. At a casual glance, Racine might seem to have gone to some pains to give an authentic picture of Imperial Rome at this period:

> Les déserts autrefois peuplés de sénateurs
> Ne sont plus habités que par leurs délateurs. (209-10)

Close inspection reveals that the number of specifically Roman terms is limited (see *28,* pp. 109-17). For example, words such as 'censeur' (271, 1096) or 'auspices' (1187) are used in a very general sense. There is not a single reference to a Roman god. Those terms which are specific to Roman life are themselves used sparingly. We are given less a picture of Rome than fleeting images of power and authority ('sénat', 'consul', 'légion', 'faisceaux', 'aigles'), together with images of constraint and freedom ('esclaves', 'affranchis', 'Vestales'). This is very much the world of the tragic action. Words which do recur more often have no particular link with Nero's Rome. An example is 'cour'. The term (twenty-three occurrences) is less a reference to a particular imperial court than an evocation of the place where one man has all power, the 'infidèle cour' (944) of spying, fawning and betrayal where the tragedy is played out, the gilded prison from which it seems the only escape is death. It is obvious, with these terms, that Racine is suggesting a certain atmosphere rather than painting a picture of Roman life.

This impression is reinforced if we examine a second set of terms relating to Roman life: 'Empire', 'Empereur', 'César', 'Rome'. These words occur with great regularity throughout the play (forty times in the first two scenes alone). They are not mere historical or geographical notations:

> Il est votre empereur. Vous êtes comme nous
> Sujette à ce pouvoir qu'il a reçu de vous. (1109-10)

As with the first set of words, none of these terms is used just to add historical colour. All are connected with the exercise

of power: 'empereur' is one with 'pouvoir'. Consider how
Néron attempts to persuade Junie to marry him:

> J'ai parcouru des yeux la cour, Rome et l'Empire.
> Plus j'ai cherché, Madame, et plus je cherche encor
> En quelles mains je dois confier ce trésor,
> Plus je vois que César, digne seul de vous plaire,
> En doit être lui seul l'heureux dépositaire,
> Et ne peut dignement vous confier qu'aux mains
> A qui Rome a commis l'empire des humains.   (576-82)

The first line alone stresses in what way Néron sees his
imperial role. He surveys the whole world from on high, like
a God. The language of the passage has an almost religious
tenor, the repetition of 'seul' and 'digne' emphasizing Néron's
monotheistic vision of the world: since from him comes all
authority, he alone is worthy of adoration. This 'César' is
beyond the mortal world, the supreme arbiter of human life,
of 'l'empire des humains'. 'Rome', 'Empire', 'César', are all
projections of a self-image: Néron master of all. Narcisse later
plays to this image with deadly effect (e.g. 'Elle a repris sur
vous son souverain empire', 1415). If *César* is not a man like
other men, why should he be bound by the laws which
govern mankind? As we shall see in the final chapter, it is on
this question that the tragic action turns.

As the play develops, the purely historical/geographical
connotations of terms such as 'César' and 'Empire' lose their
moral neutrality. Junie, abducted by Néron and a prisoner in
his palace, is the first to see that 'l'empire des humains' has
becomed the empire of Néron's desires:

> Tout ce que vous voyez conspire à vos désirs;
> Vos jours toujours sereins coulent dans les plaisirs.
> L'Empire en est pour vous l'inépuisable source.   (649-51)

Junie is thus placed before a morally significant choice when
Néron asks her to 'passer du côté de l'Empire' (588). And
some of the disturbing implications of absolute power are
expressed pithily in lines such as 'César impunément ne sera
pas jaloux' (445), 'Et jamais l'Empereur n'est absent de ces
lieux' (714) or 'L'Empereur n'a rien fait qu'on ne puisse

excuser' (822). This expression of absolutism comes to a climax in the dialogue between Néron and Britannicus which ends with the latter's arrest (Act III, Scene 8). Néron is demanding respect and obedience:

NÉRON

Si vous n'avez appris à vous laisser conduire.
Vous êtes jeune encore et l'on peut vous instruire.

BRITANNICUS

Et qui m'en instruira?

NÉRON

Tout l'Empire à la fois,
Rome.   (1043-46)

'Empire' and 'Rome' become an extension of Néron's desires, the quasi-metaphorical expression of a place where human rights become the ruler's right to do what he pleases with the humans at his disposal. For Britannicus Néron's empire is

Tout ce qu'a de cruel l'injustice et la force,
Les empoisonnements, le rapt et le divorce.   (1047-48)

It is clear, therefore, that the vocabulary of Roman life is not peripheral and ornamental. The 'Roman' terms are given all their resonance by the plot. They are part of the means of expressing the moral conflict opened up by Néron's search for power, and so form an integral part of the play's action. They are not landscape, but form part of a dynamic, harmonious whole. Maynard Mack makes the point with reference to Shakespeare: 'My subject is the world of *Hamlet*. I do not of course mean Denmark, except as Denmark is given a body by the play; and I do not mean Elizabethan England, though this is necessarily close behind the scenes. I mean simply the imaginative environment that the play asks us to enter when we read it or go to see it' (*14*, p. 30). Racine was not writing a history-book.

This is all very well, one might say. But what then of all the references to past history which sprinkle the play? Why

did Racine not stick to the present? The conflict between
Néron, Britannicus, Agrippine, Junie, the power-struggle, the
love-intrigue, is this not enough? Did we not quote Racine as
saying that 'il ne s'agit point dans ma tragédie des affaires du
dehors'? Because historical detail there certainly is! Its source,
we have seen, is often to be found in Tacitus. Its frequency
may indeed be a serious obstacle to enjoyment of the play.
Indeed, genealogical tables are *de rigueur* in most editions.
There is a constant murmur of ancestral voices, famous or
infamous: Julius Caesar, Tiberius, Caligula, Germanicus,
Agrippa, Livia and especially Augustus, the founding father,
and Claudius, the previous Emperor.

The first obvious reason for the constant recurrence of
these names from the past is the dynastic conflict between
Néron and Britannicus. Agrippine, Britannicus and Junie are
all descended from Augustus and Livia. Britannicus is the son
of Claudius. Néron is a bolt from the blue. In these circum-
stances, reference to ancestors is inevitable. 'Aïeux' is a
refrain. Authority and dignity are claimed from ancestors, the
most vocally by Agrippine:

> Et moi qui sur le trône ai suivi mes ancêtres,
> Moi, fille, femme, sœur et mère de vos maîtres.   (155-56)

Burrhus reminds the upstart Néron of the moral authority
given to Agrippine by what she calls 'les droits de mes aïeux'
(1121), suggesting that the Emperor must not underestimate
the present-day significance of these famous ancestors:

> Agrippine, Seigneur, est toujours redoutable.
> Rome et vos soldats révèrent ses aïeux.
> Germanicus son père est présent à leurs yeux.
> Elle sait son pouvoir.   (768-71)

Junie, too, 'est dans un palais tout plein de ses aïeux' (238).
This fact she uses to spurn the advances of Néron, explaining
to him that she could not possibly marry anyone other than
the son of an Emperor, and thus Britannicus:

> Ah! Seigneur, songez-vous que toute autre alliance
> Fera honte aux Césars auteurs de ma naissance?   (567-68)

This reference to her illustrious ancestry is a scarcely-veiled reminder that the present Emperor is the son of the obscure Domitius Ahenobarbus.

Junie's words suggest how past history can be exploited to assert or deny political legitimacy. Britannicus taunts Néron by calling him Domitius (1040). In a similar vein, Agrippine can compare the strength of her alliance with Britannicus, son of Claudius, with what is represented by Néron, no longer 'César' or 'Empereur':

> On verra d'un côté le fils d'un empereur
> Redemandant la foi jurée à sa famille,
> Et de Germanicus on entendra la fille;
> De l'autre l'on verra le fils d'Enobarbus.   (842-45)

To this Burrhus replies that Rome chose the adopted Néron, instead of Britannicus, just as it had in the past chosen the adopted Tiberius instead of Agrippa (861-66). The seeming constitutional seriousness of this reply is deflated when we discover from Agrippine (Act IV, Scene 2) just how this 'choice' of Néron was made. The past is an ever-present source of authority in the playing-out of the tragic action.

Past history is also used as a source of moral references. This is especially true with regard to Néron. The play opens with news of the abduction of Junie. How should this be judged? What will Néron do? What *should* Néron do? The lives of ancestors, especially those of previous Emperors, are evoked as examples to follow or avoid. In Agrippine's words, 'Pour se conduire n'a-t-il pas ses aïeux?' (162). Is Néron going to be as the great and revered Augustus, reigning with the instruments of peace, harmony and clemency? Or is he going to end as Augustus began, with war and executions (32-34)? The past is seen to weigh heavily on the present. On the one hand there is the example of Caius Caligula, whose bloody tyranny was etched on every memory, whose reign was filled with acts of arbitrary power similar to the abduction of Junie:

De Rome, pour un temps, Caïus fut les délices;
Mais sa feinte bonté se tournant en fureur,
Les délices de Rome en devinrent l'horreur.   (40-42)

On the other hand, seeming to show Néron the path of
reason, virtue and tolerance, there is the moral authority
associated with the names of Augustus, Tiberius and Germanicus. For Agrippine, Néron has these glorious examples
to choose from (163-65). For her, the lesson of the past is that
Néron cannot follow his blind desires, cannot just do as he
pleases.

Narcisse draws a completely different lesson from history.
For, as he points out to Néron (Act II, Scene 2), the past is
open to interpretation. Does his master wish to repudiate his
wife in order to marry Junie? If so, there are the examples of
Augustus and Tiberius. What is Néron waiting for?

Vous seul, jusques ici contraire à vos désirs,
N'osez par un divorce assurer vos plaisirs.   (481-82)

Narcisse chooses the same historical figures as Agrippine to
propose the opposite course of action. He subverts the idea of
moral authority into one of historical precedent. His view of
history is one which allows Néron to do whatever he wishes,
to follow his 'désirs' and 'plaisirs'. This is an ironic parallel to
Burrhus's earlier declaration, that there is no opposition
between present and past moral standards:

Mais, Madame, Néron suffit pour se conduire.
J'obéis, sans prétendre à l'honneur de l'instruire.
Sur ses aïeux, sans doute, il n'a qu'à se régler;
Pour bien faire Néron n'a qu'à se ressembler.   (215-18)

'Néron n'a qu'à se ressembler', 'Néron suffit pour se conduire': that is to say, Néron will follow in the footsteps of
previous Emperors simply by looking to himself. 'Vivez,
régnez pour vous', declares Narcisse (492) to a Néron who
sees the past as depriving him of his freedom to act. 'Quoi!
toujours enchaîné de ma gloire passée...' (1332). Néron

wishes to live in the present, to live out his desires without the past calling him to account. The past is an enemy threatening the future. How many totalitarian regimes are installed with a burning of books?

The comparison with Junie is inevitable. On her flight from the palace, after the murder of Britannicus, she stops to say a prayer at the statue of Augustus:

> Prince, par ces genoux, dit-elle, que j'embrasse,
> Protège en ce moment le reste de ta race.   (1731-32)

Junie here looks to a world beyond the world of Néron. For her, the past is not just a series of arbitrary events, open to different interpretations, which can safely be ignored. The past for her carries moral values by which the present can be judged.

References to past history are thus used by Racine to help give a moral dimension to his tragedy rather than to give it the character of a history. 'The play's the thing.' Great as was his admiration for Tacitus, Racine was, above all, a practical playwright wishing to fill his theatre 'on the night'. *Britannicus* is not a tableau of Roman history, but an evolving, dynamic structure of events made present for us. Past history is made to bear upon that present time as surely as a person's past belongs to his present, living being. (Compare the treatment of the Trojan War in Racine's previous tragedy, *Andromaque*.) What has happened long before the play begins, far from being historical anecdote, becomes a living part of the dramatic action.

What has happened in the past nourishes the fears and hopes of all. The past is seen by Agrippine with nostalgia for a power she would like to exercise anew (91-96). For Britannicus and Junie the memory of the past constantly fuels an ever-present sense of betrayal and loss. Britannicus is 'banni du rang de mes aïeux' (1489). Junie describes herself as 'Seul reste du débris d'une illustre famille' (556): she is someone 'Qui vit presque en naissant éteindre sa famille' (612).

It is ironic, therefore, that in his attempt to win over Junie, Néron should ask her to remember the past: 'Vous-même consultez vos premières années' (583). 'Du sang dont vous sortez rappelez la mémoire' (623). It is ironic, because both Junie's refusal of Néron and her love for Britannicus she places in the light of the past. In this light she finds the values by which she lives. It is impossible to miss the deliberate mingling of past and present tenses in her declaration of loyalty:

> J'aime Britannicus. Je lui fus destinée
> Quand l'Empire devait suivre son hyménée.
> Mais ces mêmes malheurs qui l'en ont écarté,
> Ses honneurs abolis, son palais déserté,
> La fuite d'une cour que sa chute a bannie,
> Sont autant de liens qui retiennent Junie.   (643-48)

Past and present are interwoven by Junie into a seamless garment of refusal.

If past history is for Junie an ever-burning flame which guides her actions, for Néron the past is seen as a present threat to the fragile moral authority of his empire. The past must be silenced, be its message voiced by Britannicus or Agrippine. Indeed, Narcisse's charge against Britannicus is that 'son cœur offensé / Prétendait tôt ou tard rappeler le passé' (1665-66). Details from the life and death of Claudius return at moments to haunt Néron, obsessed as he is that the power secured for him by Agrippine is not complete or legitimate:

> Est-ce pour obéir qu'elle l'a couronné?
> N'est-il de son pouvoir que le dépositaire?   (1234-35)

Agrippine's long account of how the son of Domitius Aheno-barbus became Emperor (1119-96) must not, therefore, be seen as some dead weight of historical lumber which, at a critical moment, delays the action of the play. What she says is at the very centre of that action. The roots of Néron's power are seen to be incest, murder and treachery. Agrippine reminds her son that he is nothing without her, that he is a usurper, that his 'Empire' has no moral authority. By placing

Néron's power in its historical context, she places it in its true
tragic perspective.

Agrippine's account of the past, however, casts fateful
shadows into the future and becomes ironic with hindsight.
For she is giving Néron a lesson with immediate practical
applications. In her dealings with Claudius, loving tenderness
has been the means to power: 'Ses gardes, son palais, son lit
m'étaient soumis' (1178). Néron is a truer son and a better
pupil than she could ever have imagined. He replaces hostility with caresses (1587-90), and then murders Britannicus
after a loving embrace (1621). His mother's policy of kiss and
kill is mockingly re-enacted. Her long historical account in
Act IV is thus a very real presence in Act V, and suggests a
not-too-distant future where she too will go the way of
Britannicus (1676-80). The past has caught up with Agrippine.

Past history, therefore, is used in a continuous and complex relationship with the present time of the play's action.
That action, as convention demanded, takes place on the one
day (Junie says in Act V, 'Je ne connais Néron et la cour que
d'un jour', 1521). In his handling of the plot, Racine exploits
this apparently crippling convention to create dramatic ex-
citement and instil a growing feeling of urgency, that time is
running out, that something must be done before it is too late:

> Mais Néron vous menace: en ce pressant danger,
> Seigneur, j'ai d'autres soins que de vous affliger. (985-86)

But our sense of time, as we watch or read *Britannicus,* is
not bounded by these few hours. References to past history
are used by Racine to expand the dimension of time allowed
him. This new dimension in time becomes one with a moral
dimension. We have noted the paradox of how references to
past history are used by Racine to give his tragedy a moral
rather than a historical character. By a related paradox, these
historical allusions take the play beyond the confines of a
particular moment in history. (A recent production of the
play was set in Nazi Germany.) Néron's world is our own.

Racine uses all his historical material to free our imagination, not to restrict it.

There is a further paradox here. This new dimension of time, this moral dimension, brings us back to Nero's Rome, re-creates it in an essential form. This is how it was, because this is how it is. It is at this precise point that Aristotle draws the dividing-line between drama and history: 'The distinction between historian and poet is not in the one writing prose and the other verse [...]; it consists really in this, that the one describes the thing that has been, and the other a kind of thing that might be. Hence poetry is something more philosophic and of greater import than history, since its statements are of the nature of universals, whereas those of history are singulars' (*8*, Ch. IX).

As the tragic action reaches a climax, the play's dimension of time stretches into the future and beyond. It is instructive to compare the treatment of Néron and Junie in the last scenes. When Agrippine confronts Néron after the murder of Britannicus, she draws together the strands of time, past, present and future, in a web which, ironically, imprisons an absolute ruler who acted to be at last free of all constraints. In a relentless sequence of future tenses (1681-92) her son is ensnared, his future mapped out, fixed on a grid:

> Et ton nom paraîtra, dans la race future,
> Aux plus cruels tyrans une cruelle injure.   (1691-92)

Néron is caught in history, his life before he has lived it fixed immovably in time. He has become a prisoner of time.

At the same moment his prisoner Junie is freed from time's contingencies. Consider the description of her escape from Néron. First she addresses the statue of Augustus, and speaks of her undying love for Britannicus:

> On veut après sa mort que je lui sois parjure;
> Mais pour lui conserver une foi toujours pure,
> Prince, je me dévoue à ces dieux immortels
> Dont ta vertu t'a fait partager les autels.   (1735-38)

The people listening take pity on her, and lead her to the Vestal temple:

> Ils la mènent au temple, où depuis tant d'années
> Au culte des autels nos vierges destinées
> Gardent fidèlement le dépôt précieux
> Du feu toujours ardent qui brûle pour les dieux. (1743-46)

'Foi toujours pure', 'dieux immortels', 'autels', 'vertu', 'fidèlement', 'feu toujours ardent qui brûle pour les dieux': the language here speaks of faith and faithfulness (compared with the 'infidèle sang' of Narcisse, 1752), virtue and innocence, the days and hours seen *sub specie aeternitatis*. Just as Junie has defied Néron with values from the past, so now she throws down the challenge of eternity. Eternity, that is, that eternal freedom of moral absolutes that no tyrant, however absolute, can touch.

Britannicus is a dance to the music of time. Even in its most detailed allusions to the world of Rome, the play brings us face to face with the inescapable reality of the moral universe. The evocation of history, the playing on our sense of time, paradoxically take us out of time, to within that timeless circle where on a stage before us, in the tragic action, are played out the desires, fears and hopes of humankind.

4

Language

T H E language of Racine has often aroused two extreme and contradictory reactions. It has been slighted as unpoetic, or else set on its own, floodlit on a pedestal, as a particularly fine specimen of pure poetry. It has been counted for nothing, or seen as everything.

The first reaction has been a common Anglo-Saxon attitude. Coming from the cosmic vision and metaphorical cornucopia of Shakespeare, we encounter a verse of seemingly monotonous rhythm, frigid conventions and impoverished imagery. In the back of our minds we might have, say, the expression of a passion such as this:

> I'll not shed her blood,
> Nor scar that whiter skin of hers than snow,
> And smooth, as monumental alabaster.
>
> (*Othello,* Act V, Scene 2)

In this case, our pulses will not immediately be set racing by a line such as 'Néron impunément ne sera pas jaloux' (445). On first hearing, it will seem a very poor relation. Small wonder that so many hapless translators, at the sharp end of Racine's language, have sought to improve on it by adding a stiff dose of 'poetry'. Charles Gildon expressed this attitude in robustly patriotic style:

> The weighty bullion of One Sterling Line,
> Drawn to French wire, would thro' whole pages shine.

(Quoted in that excellent study of Racine's language, *40*, p. 281.) In this context, even references to Racine's 'clarity' or

'simplicity' can be damning with faint praise, if this suggests
lack of complexity or imaginative fire. In all its manifesta-
tions, this first reaction is the temptation of ignorance.

The second reaction might be called the temptation of
knowledge. Here words are the whole world. Racine's language becomes a self-enclosed paradise of paradigms, where
inventive researchers toil, and severe psychologists grimly
pluck the forbidden fruit of meaning. Or perhaps, Racine's
poetry may be seized on as the key to some inner garden of
significance, overlooked by those who babble of plot and
tragedy. Eugène Vinaver, complaining with some justice that
Racine's language had not attracted enough attention, put his
own cards on the table: 'Chacun sait qu'en dehors de la
poésie racinienne, il n'y a pas en réalité de tragédie racinienne' (*39*, p. 117).

A personal temptation would be to invert Vinaver's for-
mula. Is it outrageous to affirm that *Britannicus* is a *play?*
Dramatic poetry exists for and through the dramatic action of
which it is an expression. If a playwright's use of language
does not advance the dramatic action, then his attempts to
fire the imagination are vain ornaments. (Compare, for example, the Player's Speech in *Hamlet* with the body of the play.)
Poetry in drama, like fire, is a good servant but a bad master.
One who saw this only too clearly was Jean Racine: 'On ne
peut prendre trop de précautions pour ne rien mettre sur le
théâtre qui ne soit très nécessaire. Et les plus belles scènes
sont en danger d'ennuyer, du moment qu'on les peut séparer
de l'action, et qu'elles l'interrompent au lieu de la conduire
vers sa fin' *(Préface* to *Mithridate).*

These words offer a useful perspective for Racine's use of
language. The resources of rhetoric and poetic diction are to
be exploited as an integral part of a dramatic machine set in
motion to produce a tragic action. Take again the line set,
with apparent disadvantage, against the quotation from *Othello*: 'Néron impunément ne sera pas jaloux'. Closer inspection reveals certain effects of style, which together contribute
to render a simmering sense of menace and scarcely-con-
tained fury: the slightly dislocated syntax, the placing of
'Néron' and 'jaloux' in stressed positions, the contorted

double negative, the four long syllables of 'impunément' (echoing 'Néron'). But the total impact of the line is determined by where it is and what it does in the play as a whole. Narcisse has been goading Néron, as cunningly as Iago uses Othello, with images of Britannicus successfully paying court to Junie:

> A ses moindres désirs il sait s'accommoder;
> Et peut-être déjà sait-il persuader.   (433-34)

Now he has brought his master to the boil. Néron is jealous, and intends to punish the guilty person. The music of the verse helps us to experience the intensity of the jealousy and the cold reality of the threat. The line both shares in, and contributes to, that tragic irony which is one of the major structuring forces in the play: the ruler of the world cannot control his own feelings nor those of the woman he loves. There is something frightening in the spectacle of a man with absolute power ready to strike out from frustrated desire like a child. We remember, with the savour of irony, Burrhus declaring that flatterers would have destroyed Néron: 'Dans une longue enfance ils l'auraient fait vieillir' (190). But Néron is no longer a child, he is Emperor of Rome, and wishes to use for his pleasure the present he has been given: power. 'Néron n'est plus enfant. N'est-il pas temps qu'il règne?' (159).

Néron's time has come, and we sense that the real Néron is being born: 'Néron impunément ne sera pas jaloux'. The choice here of the third-person Néron, rather than 'je' or 'César', suggests that a man is surfacing from the depths who is not the known persona. The whole line is rich in associations. Indeed, it is through its associations that it is rich. And it is only a line. The associations of the words are underpinned by the diction, sharpened by their dramatic potential and given a strong emotional charge by jealousy. The emotion is heightened for being repressed, the jealousy the more intense for the potential blackmail it involves. This one line is a portent of the tragic outcome, within a glimpse of the overall tragic perspective. The poetry serves the play. But only the play gives to the poetry its true dimension. To separate one from the other is to impoverish both. T. S. Eliot saw it well: 'I start with the assumption that if poetry is merely a decoration, an added embellishment, if it merely gives people of literary tastes the pleasure of listening to poetry at the same that they are witnessing a play, then it is superfluous. It must justify itself dramatically, and not merely be fine poetry shaped into a dramatic form'.[4]

Poetry? Yes, we might say, but why this particular kind of poetry? Why wave on lulling wave of rhyming alexandrine? And why such a refined, restricted vocabulary? Is it not all very artificial? If the dramatist wishes to represent situations of extreme conflict, why can he not use the ordinary prose of ordinary human beings? Here again Eliot tugs at our sleeve: 'Whether we use prose or verse on the stage, they are both but means to an end [...] In those prose plays which survive, which are read and produced on the stage by later generations, the prose in which the characters speak is as remote, for the best part, from the vocabulary, syntax and rhythm of our ordinary speech – with its fumbling for words, its constant recourse to approximation, its disorder, and its unfinished sentences – as verse is [...] So it will appear that prose, on the stage, is as artificial as verse: or alternatively, that verse can be as natural as prose' (ibid., p. 73).

In the sphere of artistic creation, the artificial and the natural can never be simple opposites. The terms are like confused and slightly weary fellow-travellers. Any 'artificial' medium can be accepted as 'natural' by an audience which has already accepted that all the stage is the world. All art is by definition 'artificial' in its means of expression. The actor of a 'realistic' drama who spits and swears his way across the stage is expressing an artefact no more or less than the one who speaks the rhyming alexandrines of *Britannicus*. Whatever the means, the end is the creation of a dramatic universe which gives tongue to our human complexities more truly and intensely than in the everyday. Not every form has this potential. Tragedy demands a certain 'high seriousness'. For however true to life, tragedy is not ordinary. It deals with

[4] *On Poetry and Poets* (London, Faber, 1957), p. 72.

essentials, in Jouvet's words 'un monde qui n'est pas semblable à l'autre et qui est débarrassé du médiocre et du quotidien' (*12*, p. 135). Its characters, though human beings like us, are people who face life-or-death choices, people on whose fate often hangs the destiny of nations. Its action concerns the starkest moral dilemmas of mankind.

The alexandrine has a formal dignity which makes it a suitable vehicle for this tragic action. The restriction of vocabulary is a concomitant. Any incongruity between formal rhymed verse and trivial detail would fracture the necessary decorum of the medium. Verse pattern and verbal austerity are thus not barriers for an impatient imagination, but wings on which it may take flight. They take us up beyond the confusing claims of everyday detail. They invite us to seek beyond the tired conventions and stale customs of 'the real world', perhaps to reach out to the expression of something essential in human nature. Nor must we forget that, in all art, self-imposed limitations are often a spur to creation. The restraints imposed by poetic form and choice of vocabulary are the source of other freedoms. They allow varieties of emphasis and suggestion which increase the emotional pitch, and challenge the ordinary categories of our awareness. By these means can poetry allow us to explore the 'unpath'd waters' of the human condition. 'The poetic functioning of language is in itself a symptom of and a contribution to an extension of our experience: it is, in a sense, a form of discovery, a pushing of the bounds of apprehension beyond the limits of exact observation and into areas where literal certainty and systematic knowledge do not provide the appropriate answers' (*17*, p. 12).

So much for theory. Perhaps a brief scrutiny of three extracts from *Britannicus* will give a more concrete illustration of how Racine handled three different types of dramatic discourse: a) dialogue, b) narrative and c) visionary language.

a) *Dialogue*

BRITANNICUS

Vous ne me dites rien? Quel accueil? Quelle glace!
Est-ce ainsi que vos yeux consolent ma disgrâce?
Parlez. Nous sommes seuls. Notre ennemi, trompé,
Tandis que je vous parle, est ailleurs occupé.
Ménageons les moments de cette heureuse absence.

JUNIE

Vous êtes en des lieux tout pleins de sa puissance.
Ces murs mêmes, Seigneur, peuvent avoir des yeux;
Et jamais l'Empereur n'est absent de ces lieux.

BRITANNICUS

Et depuis quand, Madame, êtes-vous si craintive?   (707-15)

This extract is taken from the first meeting of the young
lovers. Britannicus, who has not seen Junie since her abduction, has come bursting in, firing off question after question.
Junie has said nothing. Unknown to Britannicus, Néron is
hidden, watching and listening. Junie knows that the slightest
display of love, or tremor of emotion, will mean the death of
Britannicus. Néron's threat has been voiced with sibilant hiss
and monosyllabic intensity: 'Si ses jours vous sont chers,
éloignez-le de vous' (669). Out of love, Junie must be ice-cold
with the man she loves. She must prevent Britannicus from
incriminating himself, but cannot. In this scene, of which
Néron is the architect, Junie and Britannicus are condemned
to torture themselves and each other with jealousy and
despair. Néron has been unable to win over Junie. Now he
projects his jealousy on to Britannicus, as on to a screen, for
his pleasure. He exercises power over them through fear, as
his mother had done with the Senate, 'derrière un voile,
invisible et présente' (95).

In this situation each word spoken is filled with that
emotion which the plot has been designed to create. Out of
context, nothing could be more prosaic than 'Vous ne me
dites rien?' In this context, the words are vibrant with fear.

Each syllable spells out the wound of doubt opened up in Britannicus, and itself inflicts a wound on the helpless Junie, a wound on which the next exclamations come to hammer: 'Quel accueil! Quelle glace!' The words are spoken by Britannicus to himself. He cannot get through to Junie. Indeed, it is suggested that she does not even dare look at him (708). He cannot know the extent of Néron's threat ('J'entendrai des regards que vous croirez muets', 682). In the mutism of Junie's cold, averted gaze, in the disorientation of Britannicus, we sense all Néron's hidden pleasure. His rival is being tortured by the woman he loves, with him listening ('Je me fais de sa peine une image charmante', 751). Here the dramatic action is carried forward through language and absence of language. Neither Junie nor Néron speaks, but the words of Britannicus set up an intense interplay of emotion between the three characters. Language is action.

Irony gives to all Britannicus's words a dimension of terror and pity. 'Parlez'. The request is simple, its realization impossible: a single word spans the tragic void. For Junie has only one right, to speak in a way which will please Néron and offend Britannicus (683-84). This means silence. 'Nous sommes seuls'. The terseness reflects urgency and disarray. With supreme economy the language uncovers different layers of irony. In an obvious sense, Britannicus and Junie are not alone, though Britannicus is alone in his ignorance of this. But in another sense both are alone, exiles now exiled from each other by Néron, thrown back on themselves, forced to make impossible choices in the solitary confinement of their tragic situation. Here we see how difficult it is to separate plot and language, as difficult as, in Yeats's words, to tell the dancer from the dance. The solitude of the tragic hero is achieved through the plot, which twists tight the knot of emotional conflict. It is represented in a seemingly transparent language which reveals the dark world of human passions.

A grim irony invests Britannicus's confident declaration that Néron is 'trompé' and 'ailleurs occupé', though again, the words do have their truth, but we only discover this in the denouement. The gulf of ignorance which now separates

Britannicus from reality has become dangerous. His use of 'Notre ennemi' implicates both lovers, and line 711 suggests conspiracy. Junie must therefore speak, but what can she say? She is trapped in the net of Néron's threats: 'Vous n'aurez point pour moi de langages secrets' (681). She makes three short statements, each reminding Britannicus that Néron is ever-present in his own palace. With tragic inevitability, the signal she sends is clear to everyone except the intended recipient.

In one sense Junie's words are a total failure in communication. Britannicus takes them as a sign of fear (715), which of course they are, but he is unable to understand what kind of fear. This in turn causes him to say things which incriminate not just himself but Junie (717-18), Agrippine and others (722-23). His continued ignorance underlines how successful Néron has been in isolating the two lovers one from the other.

But within the unfolding tragic action Junie's words operate on another level. They present a sharp image of absolute power: 'Vous êtes en des lieux tout pleins de sa puissance'. The bare 'Vous êtes' for Britannicus builds up to the 'puissance' of Néron, a 'puissance' echoing by rhyme, and as refuting, his supposed 'absence'. The word 'lieux' seems neutral. Its recurrence in the play gives it a more sinister significance (see *27*, p. 225). It is Néron's prison-house (290, 1723), the place to which Junie has been taken by his soldiers in the middle of the night, 'comme une criminelle amenée en ces lieux' (605). Of these 'lieux' Néron is master: 'caché près de ces lieux, je vous verrai, Madame' (679). The pointing of 'lieux' and 'puissance', at the end of each hemistich of line 712, the alliteration of 'pleins' and 'puissance', together with the suggestiveness of 'lieux', give a density and force to this contrast of power and powerlessness. In the next line the word 'murs', emphasized by 'Ces' and 'mêmes', gives a physical solidity to the carceral resonance of 'lieux'. The collocation of 'murs' and 'yeux' introduces a frightening (and for us quite modern) dimension, that of the police state and Big Brother.

This movement stretches to the absolute in line 714: the 'jamais', and the reiterated 'absent', seem to close the door on hope. The respectful form 'Empereur' (Britannicus says 'Néron' or 'ennemi') is, as we glimpsed in the previous chapter, pregnant with oppressive associations. The three lines Junie speaks offer a vision of a totalitarian world, in which the 'Empereur' assumes a God-like omnipresence and omniscience. The rhyme of 'yeux...lieux' perfects the claustraphobic sense of confinement and hopelessness. Junie is depicting not just a moment but a tragic human state: persons without hope, watched over by an all-powerful ruler who is ready to extinguish life at the slightest gesture of revolt. This dark completeness of oppression is something of which we are given a heightened awareness through the language, the better to understand how complete is the final reversal. But now, with what can only be pity and fear, we witness the pathos of Junie, desperate but unable to act, and Britannicus, desperate but unable to see, with each incriminating word rushing headlong nearer to his death:

> Qu'est devenu ce cœur qui me jurait toujours
> De faire à Néron même envier nos amours? (717-18)

In this passage our emotions are aroused by a few simple words which espouse the rhythms of natural speech, and avoid obtrusive metaphor or rhetorical flourish. Through position and association, in urgency and irony, these words nourish the tragic action and are nourished by it. This constant interaction of language and drama generates a tragic vision no less rich than that produced by more obviously 'poetic' forms. In the best classical manner, Racine's is an art which conceals art.

b)   *Narrative*

> Je souhaitai son lit, dans la seule pensée
> De vous laisser au trône où je serais placée.
> Je fléchis mon orgueil, j'allais prier Pallas.
> Son maître, chaque jour caressé dans mes bras,

> Prit insensiblement dans les yeux de sa nièce
> L'amour où je voulais amener sa tendresse.
> Mais ce lien du sang qui nous joignait tous deux
> Ecartait Claudius d'un lit incestueux.
> Il n'osait épouser la fille de son frère.
> Le sénat fut séduit: une loi moins sévère
> Mit Claude dans mon lit, et Rome à mes genoux. (1127-37)

This extract is from the scene in Act IV where Agrippine confronts Néron with an account of the events which made him Emperor. In these lines she is recalling the first stage in the process, her conquest of Claudius. Agrippine's whole narrative (1115-1222) is one of the two longest speeches in Racine's theatre. It was obviously a risky enterprise for the dramatist. For his audience there is an evident danger of monotony. Racine could be accused of adding to Act IV a drab historical recapitulation which could more fittingly and concisely have been included in the exposition.

An examination of these lines gives some idea of how the danger was avoided. What is striking is the use of syntax by the playwright. Its resources are exploited to mirror the mixture of directness and deviousness which make up Agrippine's approach. Short, first-person bursts reveal her will and determination: 'Je souhaitai...Je fléchis...j'allai'. Repetition of first-person pronouns and adjectives stresses throughout not just that everything is of Agrippine's doing (this is her basic message), but that the person always uppermost in her mind is herself: 'mon orgueil...mes bras...où je voulais...mon lit... mes genoux'.

'Je souhaitai son lit': the phrase is brandished like a manifesto. Its brutal singlemindedness is accentuated by 'dans la seule pensée', and given a disquieting edge by the slight sibilant hiss of the first two lines. Placed in the middle, in stressed positions, are 'lit' and 'trône': for Agrippine the first implies the second. All this is direct. At the same time, the serpentine rhythm of lines 1130-32 shows Agrippine playing a waiting game, slowly ensnaring the emperor in sexual pleasure. Claudius's ignorance of this deliberate stealth (a process mimed by the syntax, and condensed in the single

word 'insensiblement'), coupled with Agrippine's systematic
fondling ('chaque jour caressé') and cold desire ('où je voulais
amener'), enucleates affection and any emotion from 'amour'
and 'tendresse', tingeing the terms with obscenity. Agrippine
is the prostitute of her unsuspecting uncle, and her payment
is power. It is impossible to overlook the emphasis placed on
the incestuous nature of this union: 'sa nièce...lien du sang...
lit incestueux...la fille de son frère'. Whether or not there is,
later (1587-90), an insidious reminder of the incestuous
caresses between Agrippina and the Emperor Nero which
Tacitus reports (*Annals*, XIV, chap. 2), there is no doubt that
Néron's 'empire' is the child of Agrippine's rape of Claudius.
The thrice-repeated 'lit' is seat and symbol of a lust for power
given an unnatural colouring by the incestuous means chosen
to achieve it.

    Is incest to be an obstacle to Agrippine's plans? We have a
certain wry amusement at Claudius's timorous hesitation in
making the incest open and legal: 'Il n'osait épouser...'
Agrippine has her own idea of law: 'Le sénat fut séduit'. This
abrupt, matter-of-fact statement, implying corruption and
scorn, seems to brush aside any objection to the taboo. The
curt simplicity of the syntax once more underlines the idea
that Agrippine in her quest for power recognizes no restraint,
personal, legal or moral. For her the 'loi' has always been her
own self-interest (e.g. 21, 69). 'Claude dans mon lit, et Rome
à mes genoux': this is the sweeping, triumphal realization of
the opening manifesto. The brutal cynicism of Agrippine's
desire is reflected in the short, sharp phrasing, structured to
show that 'Claude' means 'Rome', and that 'dans mon lit'
means 'à mes genoux'. The campaign announced in 'Je
souhaitai son lit' has been won. Submission, and power, are
total. Agrippine's words shed an ironic light on the tirade
against tyranny which she delivers to Néron after the murder
of Britannicus (1673-92). Everything she says here is a dou-
ble-edged sword, meaning to cut Néron down to size, but
striking at herself by belittling the restraints placed on the
exercise of power. The recapitulation of her victory is a
rehearsal for her downfall.

For the listening Néron, the message is clear, though it is not the one his mother is attempting to convey. The nostalgia for past power, which she has so often expressed, would alone be sufficient to cast doubt on the motives which now animate her. It is difficult to believe, by her own account of the past, that all her actions were undertaken to help her son, 'de vous laisser au trône où je serais placée'. Every phrase she uses can be turned against herself. An example is the term 'maître'. Agrippine employs it, as she does 'n'osait', with the relish of irony. Everything she says ('chaque jour caressé...où je voulais amener sa tendresse') shows how enslaved the master is. The Senate, like the Emperor, becomes just another conquest: 'séduit' is linked to 'caressé'. This is a calculated, open-eyed policy to dominate those who are blind to what is happening. The deeper irony, therefore, is that Agrippine cannot see the lesson she is giving to Néron. It is he who is now the 'maître' but, as the following scene shows, he will not submit to Agrippine's 'embrassements' (1305) as Claudius has done. Néron's reaction to his mother's speech is expressed sharply in the rhyme 'maîtresse'-'faiblesse'. A central theme of Agrippine's is how she kept Claudius in total subjection: 'Ses gardes, son palais, son lit m'étaient soumis' (1178). But Néron's desire has been freedom, which includes freedom from Agrippine (507).

Agrippine's lesson in domination is part of a whole pattern of terms which we see to be connected with liberty, constraint and slavery. Junie is abducted, and Britannicus arrested, as Néron strikes out for freedom. Narcisse strives to convince his master to make this freedom total by suggesting that the Romans would be lost without their chains: 'Ils adorent la main qui les tient enchaînés' (1442). This presents a chillingly modern image of a state whose citizens worship the ruler who enslaves them. In the conception of freedom which Néron pursues, it is clear that only one person can be free. After Agrippine's speech, Néron can only be even more attentive to the desire that this person be himself. Only with the denouement can we see that this destructive idea of freedom is also self-destructive.

A second lesson for Néron in the words of Agrippine is the proper use of 'caresses'. His mother has shown how power is gained by the cold exploitation of love. Later, she recounts how she used this same technique to hide the truth from Claudius before poisoning him (1175-83). Despite this, she believes she has won over Néron when, having promised to forgive Britannicus, he embraces her long and lovingly:

> Ah! si vous aviez vu par combien de caresses
> Il m'a renouvelé la foi de ses promesses!   (1587-88)

The rhyme of 'caresses' and 'promesses' affords an ironic parallel to her own treatment of Claudius: this lavish display of love is but a prelude to treachery. It is therefore a moment of pathos and foreboding for us when we hear that Néron is waiting to embrace Britannicus in a gesture of reconciliation (1566). In ironic submission to the lessons of Agrippine (and with perhaps a Racinian allusion to Judas), a kiss precedes the betrayal. There is thus considerable dramatic importance in the association between embracing and betraying which is developed in Agrippine's speech. This association is an additional unnatural dimension given to love as it is here expressed by mother and son. 'D'un regard enchanteur connaît-il le poison?', asks Néron with reference to Britannicus (429). The apparently vacuous *précieux* metaphor is given a malign reality by Agrippine and Néron. For them love and poison are one.

Even a cursory examination of this extract from Agrippine's long narrative suffices to show its total economy. The resources of language – rhythm, sound, repetition, association – are used to heighten dramatic tension and increase our sense of tragic irony. A speech designed to demonstrate to Néron what he owes his mother reveals the moral identity of Agrippine, and brings her son to the very decision she would have had him renounce. In the same movement we are shown how the achievement of absolute power ('Rome à mes genoux') requires that law and morality be mere functions of what the ruler wishes. 'Moi seul' (565) is the centre of a universe whose only circumference is desire. One characteristic of Racine's language which shines out here is the way in which the simplest words can carry the greatest tragic resonance, because even the smallest element is part of the total pattern. Each word, and the way it is spoken, is harnessed to a dramatic energy which produces a tragic vision.

c) *Visionary Language*

> Excité d'un désir curieux,
> Cette nuit je l'ai vue arriver en ces lieux,
> Triste, levant au ciel ses yeux mouillés de larmes,
> Qui brillaient au travers des flambeaux et des armes;
> Belle, sans ornements, dans le simple appareil
> D'une beauté qu'on vient d'arracher au sommeil.
> Que veux-tu? Je ne sais si cette négligence,
> Les ombres, les flambeaux, les cris et le silence,
> Et le farouche aspect de ses fiers ravisseurs,
> Relevaient de ses yeux les timides douceurs.
> Quoi qu'il en soit, ravi d'une si belle vue,
> J'ai voulu lui parler, et ma voix s'est perdue. (385-96)

This is part of a longer passage in which Néron relates to Narcisse the impact made on him by Junie, brought on his orders, by his soldiers, to his palace at night. It is a fine example of visionary language (compare *Andromaque*, 992-1006 or *Bérénice*, 301-17). Néron has seen something which has struck him dumb ('Immobile, saisi d'un long étonnement', 397). He now seeks to paint the picture that he has seen: 'je l'ai vue', 'une si belle vue'. The whole passage is an anthology-piece. It is admired as a brilliant poetic painting, or seen as a (sometimes Freudian) character-study of Néron. Racine's use of imagery has received detailed study. But it is important not to lose sight of the simple essentials. Luckily, Aristotle is always at hand to remind us of them: 'One may string together a series of characteristic speeches of the utmost finish as regards Diction and Thought, and yet fail to produce the true tragic effect' (8, Ch. VI). The imagery, therefore, will be 'successful' not because of its poetic qualities, but because its poetic qualities open up dramatic possibilities and enlarge the tragic perspective.

'Cette nuit je l'ai vue arriver en ces lieux'. The repeated demonstrative underlines the fundamental nature of the event for Néron, who seeks to relive the experience in words. Until this point in the play, his actions have been described by others in an essentially political language. His abduction of Junie has been seen in the light of political and dynastic struggles (e.g. 225-30). But now something has happened which will invest all Néron's actions with a new significance: he has fallen in love with Junie. This transformation is poignantly expressed in Junie's cry to Néron, when he orders the arrest of Britannicus: 'C'est votre frère. Hélas! c'est un amant jaloux!' (1070). Narcisse's inability to understand that something radical has changed in what motivates his master ('Vous? [...] Vous l'aimez', 383-85) leads Néron to embark on a confessional monologue. This graphic vision of desire has, therefore, a clear dramatic function, performing as it does an important shift in the plot. It is a crucial element in the evolution of what could have been a merely political struggle or historical tapestry into a tragic exploration of the limits of power and desire. This is the perspective which the language strives to express, and in which the images have their clearest focus. We can all savour the mysterious music of these lines, as one might hum a melody: 'Les ombres, les flambeaux, les cris et le silence'. But the melody is the richer for belonging to the symphony.

Néron's words are fired with a desire which seems the darker for coming to the light. It surfaces at night, in the suffocating closeness of the 'lieux' in which Junie is now the prisoner of his slightest wish. This desire is associated with darkness and flickering fire ('Les ombres, les flambeaux'), and refuses the language of human dialogue ('les cris et le silen-ce'). It finds expression in a violence scornful of weakness and is ready to crush any obstacle to its fulfilment ('armes', 'arracher', 'farouche', 'fiers ravisseurs'). The sadistic aspect of this appetite ('arracher au sommeil') is never far below the surface: 'J'aimais jusqu'à ses pleurs que je faisais couler' (402), 'va, cours le tourmenter' (754). Néron's desire is totalitarian. It is a desire to do what he wishes without constraint, expressed for him in the repeated rhyme 'désirs...plaisirs' (481-82, 649-50). It is a fire which gives an eerie, unnatural light. Like the 'flambeaux' it seems to deepen the surrounding darkness.

This cluster of images is opposed to the terms associated with Junie. These stress beauty ('Belle', 'beauté', 'une si belle vue'), grief ('Triste', 'yeux mouillés de larmes'), bareness ('sans ornements', 'simple', 'négligence') and innocent vulnerability ('arracher au sommeil', 'timides douceurs'). The stressed position of 'Triste' and 'Belle', standing alone at the head of the line, stamps these attributes with an almost absolute quality, as though over these Néron had no hold. For the language emphasizes that Néron and Junie do not belong to the same world. On Néron's side is the light from fire and steel: on Junie's, the brightness of tear-stained eyes which have a different kind of strength, 'Qui brillaient au travers des flambeaux et des armes'. On one hand, the glare of naked desire, fastened on the half-dressed young woman snatched from her sleep by a dictator's soldiers: on the other, the eyes raised to heaven.

The rhymes ('larmes...armes', 'ravisseurs...douceurs') serve to heighten the intensity of this opposition. Néron presides over the visible apparatus of total power: Junie has nothing, save beauty and grief. This stark contrast has an irreducible moral dimension. The world of Néron and the world of Junie share only – but here the whole plot finds its spring – the fate of Britannicus. Otherwise these worlds cannot meet. Aptly, Junie leaves Néron speechless: 'J'ai voulu lui parler et ma voix s'est perdue'. Power and helplessness, desire and refusal, have no common language, no communication except in violence, which is the death of language.

Following this encounter Néron directs all his energies to possessing the woman he desires: 'je souffre trop, éloigné de Junie' (799). The language in which the encounter has been described illustrates the abyss set between desire and possession by Junie's very helplessness and grief:

> Fidèle à sa douleur et dans l'ombre enfermée,
> Elle se dérobait même à sa renommée;

> Et c'est cette vertu, si nouvelle à la cour,
> Dont la persévérance irrite mon amour.   (415-18)

This Néron can see, yet cannot understand. Everything he does to gain Junie widens the chasm between them. Néron's blindness to human nature is placed in counterpoint to his desire to know all and to see all (682). Such is the stuff of tragic irony.

A characteristic of these three passages is the number of allusions to knowledge and ignorance, revelation and secrecy, truth and illusion, sight and blindness, light and darkness, the tension between the wish to know and the desire to hide. Such images occur throughout *Britannicus*. This opposition becomes an organizing principle of the play. It provides both the framework for the plot and a major ironic dimension of the tragic action. In a sense, this is unsurprising. We, as spectators, have come to see, we want to know. Secrets are stripped away, what has been hidden is brought out into the open. A play is a moment of truth: in a tragedy, that truth hurts. Irony and pathos are generated by our seeing what characters cannot see. The abundance in *Britannicus* of what one might call the vocabulary of truth must always, therefore, be set within the natural focus of its dramatic function.

For example, there are many terms related to secrecy. These are connected with the exercise of power. The relationship between the ideas nourishes the dramatic momentum from the beginning. Agrippine has fallen from the position where she was the hidden force behind everything, 'l'âme toute-puissante' (96), to where, as we see in the first lines of the play, she is standing outside Néron's locked door, attempting to discover what is going on: 'Surprenons, s'il se peut, les secrets de son âme' (127). This desire to know is seemingly fulfilled when, after the confrontation of Act IV, Scene 2, Agrippine appears to regain her influence with Néron. Her boast that the Emperor shares with her 'Des secrets d'où dépend le destin des humains' (1598) is made, ironically, while the destiny of Britannicus is being decided by Néron's poison. But Agrippine is not the only object of this irony. We have seen, in the first passage, Britannicus wishing to know the truth about Junie, and a God-like Néron spying on them both, thinking that nothing escapes him. A sign of Britannicus's helplessness is that Néron can seemingly read his thoughts: 'Comme toi, dans mon cœur il sait ce qui se passe' (335). Knowledge is power. Fittingly, therefore, the disclosure of secrets (as we saw in the second passage) is bound up with an uncovering of the roots of power.

This dramatic movement is set in ironic contrast with characters' blindness. The multitude of visual terms in *Britannicus* has excited the interest of many commentators (see *44,* note 23). Some see Néron and Agrippine as having a power residing in their eyes. Some consider Racine to be obsessed by the visual. Others, who refrain from apportioning extraordinary physical characteristics to characters, or indulging in any philosophical mix of the ocular and oracular, have clearly demonstrated the link which exists between sight and power. It is always necessary, however, to situate this visual language within the ironic structure of the tragic action. In passage c), for example, we see Junie stripped bare by Néron's gaze, but in a sense beyond its power, 'levant au ciel ses yeux mouillés de larmes'. All the visual language of the play, all allusions to secrecy, knowledge and power, find their significance in our discovery of tragic blindness. In this last passage as in the play as a whole, we witness an emperor all-powerful, but unable to see that power is circumscribed by human dignity.

Thus we see that Racine's poetry, even at its most openly evocative, is not something grafted on to the drama to add 'beauty' or 'colour' or 'atmosphere'. It is not composed of autonomous moments of creative brilliance, nor is it even (but perhaps this, again, is provocative) a scroll of cryptic fragments to be decoded for prospective examination candidates. Racine was a playwright. The images he uses are given life by all their associations throughout the play, and by the dramatic moment they express, just as they in turn give intensity and vision to that moment. All the poetic techniques work because literally they are working, in a dynamic dramatic machine composed to give pleasure.

A short introduction to the play is no place to give more than a cursory idea of such techniques. We have already caught a glimpse of Racine at work. He is above all a master of rhythm, constantly modulated to achieve the desired effect. Some examples (the stresses of the word-order and sound-values are, of course, always accompanying factors) are the use of repetition ('Madame, en le voyant, songez que je vous voi', 690), with the stress sometimes falling on the change of tense and subject ('J'obéissais alors, et vous obéissez', 1042) or on change of tense and complement ('Craint de tout l'univers, il vous faudra tout craindre', 1352); antithesis ('J'embrasse mon rival, mais c'est pour l'étouffer', 1314); enumeration ('Moi, fille, femme, sœur et mère de vos maîtres', 156); paradox ('Je la voudrais haïr avec tranquillité', 942); the alignment of monosyllables ('Dans le fond de ton cœur je sais que tu me hais', 1677) or syllabic contrasts ('Et laver dans le sang vos bras ensanglantés', 1346). The shift of caesura (e.g. 1536-38), the delaying of the verb (e.g. 111-12), the short sentence (e.g. 1755), chiasmus (e.g. 609-10), interrogations (e.g. 1432-36), imperatives (e.g. 1567-68), interruptions (e.g. 998), exclamations (e.g. 1541-54) and sharp exchanges (e.g. 1041-69), are some additional ways in which the pitch and tone of emotion can be changed as the plot demands. But we must not confuse the instruments with the symphony. The attempt to track down poetic devices can be desiccating, if we do not see them always at the service of the dramatic action.

It is for this reason that any study of Racine's language must begin and end with the play. For Hamlet a play was 'a fiction, a dream of passion' (*Hamlet,* Act II, Scene 2). This need not be pejorative. It is through the working-out of that fiction, to recreate that dream, that words are invested with passion. And so those words act. From the very beginning of the play – Albine's 'Quoi!' – we are plunged into a world where tensions and conflicts are sharpened to create violent emotion. The power of the emotion so created, when harnessed to various techniques of expression, can fire cold images, can give resonance and energy to the simplest words. Witness the last meeting of the lovers, with Britannicus explaining how a forgiving Néron wants publicly to embrace him:

BRITANNICUS

D'où vient qu'en m'écoutant, vos yeux, vos tristes yeux,
Avec de longs regards se tournent vers les cieux?
Qu'est-ce que vous craignez?

JUNIE

Je l'ignore moi-même,
Mais je crains.   (1501-4)

It would be possible to explain how the associations of certain words, the use of different rhythms and sounds, combine with irony to express the pathos and longing, pity and fear, with which this moment is pregnant. In the end, however, whole libraries of explanations leave us as far from seizing the mystery of that music and dance of emotion as we are from freezing fire. That fire can seize us, if only we can sit back and enjoy the play: 'on n'analyse que d'une manière bien imparfaite les œuvres de ce même génie; il faut surtout les sentir' (*4,* Vol. VIII, p. xxx). It is reassuring that in an age of ever more complex critical utterances, we still stumble to capture the hidden harmonics of Racine's music. And yet his language could not be more clear, clear as a Mozart sonata, reminding us that simplicity is the last refuge of a genius.

5

Tragedy

T H E R E is no shortage of books on tragedy. Both word and genre are undisciplined, protean beasts, difficult to fence in. So it is hardly surprising that there has been little agreement as to what constitutes the tragedy of *Britannicus* (see *44*, notes 1-4). Is the tragedy even tragic? It has been viewed as a political power-struggle, a 'slice of life' at Louis XIV's Court, a Freudian fable or a Jansenist analogue. Some deny the play tragic status because of a supposed lack of moral transcendence (i.e. violence wins), or because it projects some pre-existentialist vision of the absurd. On the other hand, many of those who do not disavow the title, '*Britannicus,* tragédie', see the tragedy as residing in the apparent horror and despair of its world-picture.

Against these views should be set the evidence we have already seen: that *Britannicus* is a play with a particular and deliberately-contrived type of plot and language. If the play is a tragedy, then its tragic character will depend on the construction of the plot and the language which sustains it. 'Tragic' in this context can never be a simple synonym for 'violent' or 'pessimistic'.

Racine did not stumble by chance on his idea of tragedy. He was an admirer of Sophocles and a discerning commentator of Aristotle. In that Greek tragedy of which Sophocles' *Oedipus Rex* is perhaps the finest flowering, Aristotle identified what he saw as an archetypal tragic pattern: initial error (*hamartia*), reversal of intention (*peripeteia*) and discovery. An act is committed, often an act which overturns some existing order. Its consequences are the opposite of that which the agent intended. This ironic reversal allows us to discover something of the inescapable nature of our human condition (*13*, p. 12). Racine follows this pattern in *Britannicus*. It is a key to understanding the real tragic nature of the play. For actions which in the everyday might be seen as gratuitous (we speak of 'blind violence') are given a certain order through the reversal and discovery effected by the plot. However horror-drenched the actions, this order implies a moral perspective.

It is only too easy to confuse moral and moralistic. The example of *King Lear* is instructive. An English contemporary of Racine, Nahum Tate, found its horror unbearable, and its ending contrary to natural justice. So he produced a more palatable play, which for a century and a half held the stage at the expense of Shakespeare's own creation.[5] In this version Lear and Cordelia are rescued by Edgar, thus proving (as the final line triumphantly states) that 'Truth and Vertue shall at last succeed'. Today this tradition is alive and kicking, not least in Hollywood. What Tate with his moralizing designs failed to see, however, is that in Shakespeare's play Goneril and Regan have a lust for power which rebounds on them, and that in Lear's suffering and Cordelia's tears is affirmed the inalienable dignity of the human spirit. Racine is not, for his part, any more than Shakespeare, a teacher of morality. He is a playwright who allows us, through the mystery of the theatrical illusion, in the paradoxical tragic pleasure of pity and fear, to become explorers of our human condition, exploring hidden relationships. The tragic action is a moment of disclosure.

In *Britannicus* that moment begins at the beginning, with Néron's abduction of Junie. This assertion of might over right triggers off a series of reactions which follow one upon the other until the reversal of Néron's original intention, when Junie escapes him for ever. With the hindsight of the denouement we can see that the play's reversal and discovery stand in direct relationship to Néron's initial error of judgement. The abduction is the signal that he is prepared to throw off the moral constraints placed on those who wield power: 'L'impatient Néron cesse de se contraindre' (11). It is an act

---

[5] *The History of King Lear... Revived with Alterations* (London, 1681).

which sets a challenge. Are there no limits? Does Néron not have to acknowledge any law beyond himself? Is there in the world no order which transcends the brutalizing appetites of mankind? The death of Britannicus, the total power which Néron seems to achieve, our knowledge of his future crimes, all appear to make for a negative answer. That is the appearance. Most of us already know the story of Nero. But Racine has transformed the story into a play. And as the play unfolds so the appearance gives way to a reality the more forceful for being hidden. Our own expectations, no less than those of the tragic protagonists, are subject to ironic reversal. What could be more natural? The play is written and performed for us. Its discovery is our discovery.

The opening scenes pose the question of power. Néron's prestige and authority are stressed, while his rivals fall about in disarray. Agrippine is kept waiting in front of the Emperor's closed door, while Britannicus can only lament his own enslavement (319-24). The Emperor seems to have everything: 'Néron jouit de tout' (67). He is the potential 'empereur parfait' (26). Freedom and justice are said by Burrhus to be the first-fruits of his reign (200-10). He is presented as father of the nation (29, 47), a man seemingly blessed by fortune (381). No different, at the beginning, was King Oedipus. This image of Néron is naturally a reflection of what has happened in the past. With the abduction we are hurled into the present. Néron has acted in the night. How will his action appear in the light of day?

First light brings Agrippine's charge that the benign image of Néron is false (35). She desires to know the truth. But what kind of truth is she after? The abduction of Junie has revived all Agrippine's fears for her own position, once so influential (91-114). Now she challenges her son, that he put his authority to the test alongside hers. Néron's act has posed the question of where real power lies. The question seems simple, the answer inevitable: as Stalin reportedly said, how many armoured divisions has the Pope? But once the question is asked, a process of discovery begins. We are set on course, as in so much theatre from the earliest of plays, for the moment the mask is stripped away, to reveal, not here the real identity

of a person, but the moral reality of actions. The abduction
seems to be a straightforward police action, a banal affirma-
tion of power. In reality it catches those jousting for power,
Agrippine and Néron, in a mechanism they can no longer
control. The *machine infernale* of the tragic plot is of its very
essence a creator of irony.

As was noted in the previous chapter, the ironies which
invest the description of Junie's arrival at the palace
(385-408) give us our first inkling that the power which
Néron so obviously commands ('Je le veux, je l'ordonne',
369) is not as total as it appears. His obsessive recapitulation
of the initial act of abduction not only serves to underline its
prime importance for the structure of the plot. Néron's words
show that he has become a prisoner of desire: 'Excité d'un
désir curieux...' This desire sets up a relationship of dependence with his prisoner Junie. All his efforts to disentangle
himself by assertions of mastery only trap him more completely in the dark labyrinths of passion. This is, again, not
what at first sight appears to be the case. It seems that Néron,
surrounded by his soldiers, can do what he wants with a
young woman whose tears are a measure of her vulnerability.
But what can he do? Ironically, the master of the universe is
reduced to the lone rehearsal of a fantasy-scene in his own
room:

> C'est là que solitaire,
> De son image en vain j'ai voulu me distraire:
> Trop présente à mes yeux je croyais lui parler;
> J'aimais jusqu'à ses pleurs que je faisais couler.   (399-402)

Néron is all-powerful in the empire of his imagination. The
term 'image' is both a token of his blindness and a symptom
of his frustration. Blinded by desire, he stands powerless
before Junie.

Blindness and desire: in Néron's actions the two become
as one. This blindness springs from the all-embracing nature
of his desire. His love for Junie is a powerful expression of the
totalitarian dream: domination not just of bodies but of hearts
and minds. Néron pursues a self-image which Narcisse is only

too ready to reflect for his master's pleasure: an emperor beyond the reach of mortal men, a king of kings, a proper object of worship for the eyes of all (449-58). This quasi-divine image contains another fantasy-picture, of a Junie dazzled by the effulgence of imperial power, her eyes suddenly opened to the truth:

> Mais aujourd'hui, Seigneur, que ses yeux dessillés
> Regardant de plus près l'éclat dont vous brillez...   (449-50)

The 'truth' is expressed concisely by Narcisse: 'Commandez qu'on vous aime, et vous serez aimé' (458). This absolutist illusion is threatened by Junie's 'vertu' (417), by her equation of Néron's 'honneurs' with 'ignominie' (424). Frustration of desire engenders in Néron the desire to remove the source of this frustration. It is a further ironic display of blindness: 'Néron impunément ne sera pas jaloux' (445). And so the error contained in the initial act of abduction is magnified. Néron's desire to know the whole truth about Junie and Britannicus, as exemplified in his decision to spy on them ('J'entendrai des regards que vous croirez muets', 682), stands in ironic contrast to the illusion he pursues with ever-greater vigour. This paradox is, as Eric Bentley saw, at the very heart of the tragic form: 'The natural wish to know is generally thwarted by the absence of any corresponding wish to face reality, the contradiction being the source of one of the archetypal tragic conflicts, classically presented by Sophocles in his *Oedipus Rex*' (*9*, p. 260).

'Qui vous arrête?' Narcisse's question to Néron (460) is another fundamental element in the tragic experience. In the totalitarian logic of the abduction, the question is natural. Néron's reply shows that he is alive merely to the possibility of material limitations. For him the achievement of total power is conditional only on the removal of certain physical obstacles, among others that of 'l'implacable Agrippine' (483). He wishes to free himself from the state of 'dépendance' (507). But he fails to see another reality. The impediment which he cannot remove is the state of dependence to which he is reduced not merely by his desire for Junie but by the human condition itself. He who is free of this dependence is either a God, or a monster.

A being beyond the ordinary world of men: this is the claim implicit in Néron's attempt to win over Junie (Act II, Scene 3). He sees himself, 'moi seul', as responsible for her destiny. He alone can be the possible object of her love because he alone is the source of power: he and the universe are one. Such infatuation is again part of a traditional tragic pattern, in which he who would play God with other men becomes a monster for mankind. This is the nub of the tragedy. We now see why Racine has selected for his drama this particular moment in Néron's life. It is the moment of choice, the beginning of Néron's descent into the monstrous: 'En un mot, c'est ici un monstre naissant' (*Seconde Préface*). It is a caricature of the tragic merely to assimilate it to the monstrous. For central to the tragic experience is our developing awareness of a moral order by which we judge the monstrous for what it is, and set it in its true human dimension.

The role of Junie is a crucial factor in this awareness. Her deflating rejection of Néron's advances ('Ni cet excès d'honneur, ni cette indignité', 610) proclaims the human indignity of the imperial 'dignité' to which Néron obsessively refers (579-602). Junie's words suggest the existence of two sets of values, only one of which has any moral worth:

> Je sais de vos présents mesurer la grandeur;
> Mais plus ce rang sur moi répandrait de splendeur,
> Plus il me ferait honte... (629-31)

The confrontation between Néron and Junie is a contrast between two worlds. Here the conflict between light and dark is perhaps not what we might expect. For it is Néron who reigns in a world of shining light, of 'éclat', 'clarté' and 'splendeur'. Junie and Britannicus have been thrown into the night, 'cette nuit profonde' (615), into a darkness equated with suffering (415, 613). 'Tout l'univers' is for Néron (653), whereas Junie has no family (612) and 'Britannicus est seul' (655). While Britannicus lives in visible disgrace (646-47),

Néron enjoys every possible gratification. The antithesis of
the two worlds develops the paradox of vulnerability already
implicit in the abduction – scene. In the 'Empire', the world
of temporal power, Néron will, like God (and by the agency
of spies like Narcisse) seem to see everything, hear everything
and know everything: 'Et jamais l'Empereur n'est absent de
ces lieux' (714). We have seen how the spy-scene (Act Two,
Scene 6) enacts this totalitarian triumph with sinister intensity: even Junie's eyes cannot communicate her feelings. Of
his empire, which ironically is shrivelled into the narrow,
closed world of his own desires, Néron is master: 'Tout ce que
vous voyez conspire à vos désirs' (649). There is no surprise
in his ascent to power.

   But Junie points us to another world, utterly beyond
Néron's reach. It is a land of suffering, solitude and helplessness, 'autant de liens qui retiennent Junie' (648). This is the
homeland of all Junie's loyalties, and here her love has its
roots. From this land Néron is cut off, as by a river of tears:
'Et ce sont ces plaisirs et ces pleurs que j'envie' (659). In his
wish to know everything Néron is blinded to that simple
human reality. This irony is compounded by another: every
step he takes to eliminate the obstacles between Junie and
himself only widens the gulf between them.

   Agrippine makes the same mistake as Néron. Power she
equates with domination, gained and maintained if necessary
by 'exils, assassinats, / Poison même' (853-54). Mother and
son are bound together by what are in every sense ties of
blood. Agrippine, like Néron, sees love in terms of power.
The Emperor's love for Junie makes the young princess as
threatening a rival for her as Britannicus is for Néron: 'Elle
aura le pouvoir d'épouse et de maîtresse' (888). It is in her
interest that Britannicus should be allowed to wed Junie. Her
struggle with Néron is by no means ideological. Mother and
son are locked in conflict because essentially they seek the
same kind of power. This is why, as we have seen, the whole
of Agrippine's long speech to Néron (Act IV, Scene 2) is
coloured with unconscious irony. Her words are of course
important in themselves. They show how the proud arch of
Néron's empire has been established on the noble pillars of

his mother's sexual despotism and the praetorian guard (1178-92). But this is not the main discovery to which we have been moving from the beginning of the play. Agrippine has the same ironic relationship to the play's real discovery as Néron, because she shares the same blindness. She imagines that she can see through her son (1269): this is illusion enough. But, more importantly, she has been unable to see that the lust for total power can spawn a monster. The play's tragic action, set in motion by the abduction of Junie, moves irreversibly towards the discovery, not just of the monstrous, but also of its limits.

On the surface such limits might seem to exist more in idealist rhetoric than in reality. For Racine cannot be accused of concessions to easy sentiment. The more often critics have suggested that *Britannicus* ends in black despair. Néron's world is unquestionably harsh, its lingua franca the silent language of submission. Thus the poignancy of Britannicus's despairing question: 'L'amour est-il muet, ou n'a-t-il qu'un langage?' (996). Néron spells out to his rival (Act III, Scene 8) a whole grammar based on respect, obedience, punishment, silence and fear: 'il suffit qu'on me craigne' (1056). His language in this scene has, for us, the bleakly familiar ring of totalitarian terror. This is the world of torture and concentration camps, of night arrests and easy murder. Total freedom for one man, to do as he wishes, means the total enslavement of all others: as Lord Acton's famous phrase reminds us, absolute power corrupts absolutely. Agrippine has been able to see this truth only in terms of narrow self-interest, while Burrhus, who has defended the abduction of Junie, wakes up too late to the implications of Néron's desire to 's'affranchir' (802). For Néron the assassination of Britannicus is a question of freedom. Why should he be shackled by others?

> Soumis à tous leurs vœux, à mes désirs contraire,
> Suis-je leur empereur seulement pour leur plaire?   (1335-36)

It is no coincidence that when Narcisse sets out to overturn the counsels of reconciliation proffered by Burrhus, the trigger words he uses to convince Néron are 'empire', 'désir'

and 'libre'. Nothing better illustrates Touchard's remark that
'les conversations de Néron et de Narcisse [...] sont comme un
dialogue entre le conscient et l'inconscient' (*22,* p. 99).
Narcisse first puts in his master's mind the idea that peace
with Britannicus means surrender to the 'souverain empire'
of Agrippine (1415). Has Néron not forgotten the most
important person? 'De vos propres désirs perdrez-vous la
mémoire?' (1435). Then Narcisse goes straight to the heart of
the matter. Britannicus must be killed: 'Vous seriez libre
alors, Seigneur' (1465). Néron is placed before a choice:
either the kingdom of his unfettered desires, or an 'Empire'
existing only in name, a 'spectacle', a pathetic illusion of
power performed by a ham actor before an incredulous
audience (1474-78). Narcisse reminds his master that there is
only one language, the language of power and desire. This
can belong to one man alone: 'Ah! ne voulez-vous pas les
forcer à se taire?' (1479). Néron accepts this invitation to
silence Britannicus. In this act of liberation he seeks to free
himself from the constraints which govern the human condition.

This murder is the logical and inexorable continuation of
the mechanism set in motion by the abduction of Junie. It is
an act which immediately provokes reversal and then discovery. Néron's initial error now rebounds on him. With the
irony proper to tragedy, the Emperor's desire is frustrated by
the very action designed to lead to its consummation. The
attempt to remove the final obstacle to Junie deprives Néron
eternally of her. That prefatory assertion of power and desire,
the abduction, is seen now to have precipitated a chain of
events which has overturned the original intention, showing
the vanity of this power and the futility of the desire. Even
the supreme power, that of life and death, crumbles before
Néron's very eyes. This is the message of Agrippine's defiant
cry: 'je veux que ma mort te soit même inutile' (1679).
Néron's imagined 'Empire' is suddenly overturned and, with
the play's discovery, we are brought into another realm.

This is not merely a question of Agrippine's recognition
of the monster which her own actions have created. The final
scene makes it clear that the play's discovery is ours. We see

an emperor who has lost his way: 'Il marche sans dessein' (1757). The language of imperial brilliance is quite extinguished. Ascribed to Néron is the same vocabulary of exile as was previously employed for Britannicus and Junie: 'nuit', 'solitude', 'désespoir', 'inquiétude', 'douleur'. We have a vision of Néron stumbling back into the dark night in which he committed the initial tragic error of the abduction:

> Et l'on craint, si la nuit jointe à la solitude
> Vient de son désespoir aigrir l'inquiétude,
> Si vous l'abandonnez plus longtemps sans secours,
> Que sa douleur bientôt n'attente sur ses jours. (1759-62)

Such is the universe gained by the God-like Emperor: a suggestion of madness in those all-seeing eyes ('ses yeux mal assurés [...] leurs regards égarés', 1757-58), and a prophetic hint of suicide. The reversal is complete. The play's tragic structure, with this discovery, is now completely unfolded. An order is restored which had been violated by one who acted as though no order existed save his own.

A recognition of this tragic pattern challenges those interpretations which see the play ending with night covering the face of the earth. It is true that the last line reminds us of horrors to come. But can *Britannicus,* taken as a whole, be seen as the account of a seizure of power or as a chronicle of the monstrous? These elements certainly exist, but they subsist in something greater, which we might call a tragic vision. This is the focus, this the magnetic pole to which we have seen Racine's craft bend. The choice and invention of material, the construction of the plot, the use of history, the music of the language, the whole structure of the play, from initial error to reversal and discovery, all of these combine to give to the dramatic action a tragic dimension which involves a sense of moral order.

Aristotle describes Oedipus as having accomplished his initial deed of horror 'in ignorance of his relationship' (*8*, Ch. XIV). Similarly, in abducting Junie, Néron acts in ignorance of his human relationship. This is the beginning of his seizure of total power. It is also the beginning of a tragedy which for us is very much a voyage of discovery. Through the playing-out of the tragic action we discover that no man, however free or powerful, can free himself from the moral order of the human condition. In the tragic experience and the emotions it arouses we gain a heightened awareness of what is meant by our common humanity.

Néron is shown to be a human being. It is for each of us to judge whether this provides grounds for optimism or pessimism, or indeed, whether terms such as these can adequately describe the living experience of great tragedy.

Select Bibliography

T H E bibliography of Racine is monumental. The following does not pretend to be a representative sample. It attempts to list works which have been found helpful: direct reference has not been made to all of them in the preceding pages.

EDITIONS

1. *Britannicus,* ed. J.-P. Caput (Paris, Larousse, 1970). (Easily available.)
2. *Britannicus,* ed. P. Butler (Cambridge, Cambridge University Press, 1967).
3. *Britannicus,* ed. W. H. Barber (London, Macmillan, 1967).
4. *Œuvres,* ed. P. Mesnard (Paris, Hachette, 1865-73). 8 vols and 2 albums. (*Britannicus* in Vol. II: the indispensable edition.)
5. *Œuvres complètes,* ed. R. Picard (Paris, Gallimard, Bibl. de la Pléiade, 1950). 2 vols. (*Britannicus* in vol. I: excellent Introduction and notes.)
6. *Théâtre complet,* ed. J. Morel and A. Viala (Paris, Garnier, 1980). (N.B. The line-numbering of *Britannicus* in this edition goes awry from line 1060 onwards.)

BACKGROUND AND SOURCES

7. Adam, A., *Histoire de la littérature française au XVIIe siècle* (Paris, Domat, 1948-56). 5 vols.
8. Aristotle, *Poetics,* trans. Ingram Bywater (Oxford, Clarendon Press, 1920).
9. Bentley, E., *The Life of the Drama* (London, Methuen, 1965).
10. Bray, R., *La Formation de la doctrine classique en France* (Paris, Hachette, 1927; Nizet, 1957).
11. Griffin, M., *Nero: The End of a Dynasty* (London, Batsford, 1984).
12. Jouvet, L., *Témoignages sur le théâtre* (Paris, Flammarion, 1952).
13. Krook, D., *Elements of Tragedy* (New Haven, Yale University Press, 1971).

14. Mack, M., 'The world of *Hamlet'* in Brooks, C., (ed.), *Tragic Themes in Western Literature* (New Haven, Yale University Press, 1955), pp. 30-58.
15. Moore, W., *The Classical Drama of France* (Oxford University Press, 1971).
16. Morel, J., *La Tragédie* (Paris, Armand Colin, 1964).
17. Prior, M., *The Language of Tragedy* (New York, Columbia University Press, 1947).
18. Scherer, J., *La Dramaturgie classique en France* (Paris, Nisard, 1950).
19. Sedgewick, G., *Of Irony especially in Drama* (Toronto University Press, 1948).
20. Suetonius, *The Twelve Caesars,* translated by R. Graves (London, Cassell, 1957).
21. Tacitus, *Annals,* trans. G. Ramsay (London, John Murray, 1904-09).
22. Touchard, P.-A., *Le Théâtre et l'angoisse des hommes* (Paris, Seuil, 1968).
23. Truchet, J., *La Tragédie classique en France* (Paris, P.U.F., 1975).
24. Vinaver, E., *Principes de la tragédie en marge de la Poétique d'Aristote* (Manchester University Press, 1944).

RACINE

25. Barnwell, H. T., *The Tragic Drama of Corneille and Racine* (Oxford, Clarendon Press, 1982).
26. Barthes, R., *Sur Racine* (Paris, Seuil, 1963).
27. Bernet, C., *Le Vocabulaire des tragédies de Jean Racine* (Geneva, Slatkine, 1983).
28. Cahen, J.-C., *Le Vocabulaire de Racine* (Paris, Droz, 1946).
29. France, P., *Racine's Rhetoric* (Oxford, Clarendon Press, 1965).
30. Goldmann, L., *Racine* (Paris, L'Arche, 1956).
31. Haley, Sr M., 'Peripeteia and Recognition in Racine', *Publications of the Modern Language Association of America,* XV (1940), 426-39.
32. Mauron, C., *L'Inconscient dans l'œuvre et la vie de Racine* (Aix-en-Provence, Publications des Annales de la Faculté des Lettres, 1957).
33. May, G., *Tragédie cornélienne, tragédie racinienne* (Urbana, University of Illinois Press, 1948).
34. Mourgues, O. de, *Racine or, The Triumph of Relevance* (Cambridge, Cambridge University Press, 1969).
35. Niderst, A., *Les Tragédies de Racine* (Paris, Nizet, 1975).
36. Picard, R., *La Carrière de Jean Racine* (Paris, Gallimard, 1956).
37. Scherer, J., *Racine et/ou la cérémonie* (Paris, P.U.F., 1982).
38. Vinaver, E., *Racine et la poésie tragique* (Paris, Nizet, 1951).
39. ———, *Entretiens sur Racine* (Paris, Nizet, 1984).
40. Wheatley, K., *Racine and English Classicism* (Austin, University of Texas Press, 1969).

PARTICULAR STUDIES ON 'BRITANNICUS'

41. Ault, H., 'The Tragic Protagonist and the Tragic Subject in *Britannicus*', *French Studies*, IX (1955), 18-29.

42. Bonnet, P., 'Les diverses manières d'appeler Néron dans *Britannicus*', *Jeunesse de Racine*, 1969, 44-48.

43. Brody, J., 'Les yeux de César: the language of vision in *Britannicus'* in *Studies in Seventeenth Century French Literature Presented to Morris Bishop* (Ithaca, Cornell University Press, 1962), 185-201.

44. Campbell, J., 'The Tragedy of *Britannicus'*, *French Studies*, XXXVII (1983), 391-403.

45. Cook, A., 'Displacement and condensation in *Britannicus'* in *French Tragedy: the power of enactment* (Chicago-London, Swallow Press, 1981), 1-25.

46. Couton, G., '*Britannicus*, tragédie des cabales', in *Mélanges d'histoire littéraire offerts à Raymond Lebègue* (Paris, Nizet, 1969), 269-77.

47. Doubrovsky, S., 'L'arrivée de Junie dans *Britannicus*: la tragédie d'une scène à l'autre', *Papers on French Seventeenth Century Literature*, 10 (1978-79), 223-66.

48. Gutwirth, M., '*Britannicus*, tragédie de qui?', in *Racine: mythes et réalités* (London, Ontario, University of Western Ontario, 1976), 53-69.

49. Hartle, R., *Index des mots de 'Britannicus'* (Paris, Klincksieck, 1956).

50. Jasinski, R., 'Sur deux vers de *Britannicus* (155-56)' in *A travers le XVIIe siècle*, 2 vols (Paris, Nizet, 1981), II, 14-21.

51. Miquel, J.-P., 'A propos d'une mise en scène de *Britannicus'*, *Cahiers de l'Association Internationale des Etudes Françaises*, 31 (1979), 135-48.

52. Moore, W., *Racine: Britannicus* (London, Arnold, 1960).

53. Sweetser, M.-O., 'Racine rival de Corneille: "innutrition" et innovation dans *Britannicus'*, *Romanic Review*, LXVI (1975), 13-31.

54. Tans, J., 'Un thème-clé racinien: la rencontre nocturne', *Revue d'Histoire Littéraire de la France*, LXV (1965), 577-89.

55. Tobin, R., 'Néron et Junie: fantasme et tragédie', *Papers on French Seventeenth Century Literature*, 19 (1983), 681-99.

56. Van Delft, L., 'Language and power: eyes and words in *Britannicus'*, *Yale French Studies*, 45 (1970), 102-12.

57. Venesoen, C., 'Le Néron de Racine: un cas curieux d'impuissance verbale', *L'Information Littéraire*, XXXI (1981), 130-36.

58. Woshinsky, B., 'Intuition in *Britannicus'*, *Analecta Husserliana*, XVIII (1984), 1-25.

59. Zimmerman, E., 'La lumière et la voix: étude sur l'unité de *Britannicus'*, *Revue des Sciences Humaines*, XXXIII (1968), 169-83.

CRITICAL GUIDES TO FRENCH TEXTS

edited by
Roger Little, Wolfgang van Emden, David Williams